THE
Sparkle Factory

The Design and Craft of Tarina's
Fashion Jewelry and Accessories

TARINA
TARANTINO

RUNNING PRESS
PHILADELPHIA · LONDON

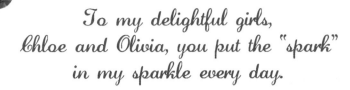

To my delightful girls,
Chloe and Olivia, you put the "spark"
in my sparkle every day.

To my beautiful friend, Alyssa,
you have inspired me more than you will ever know.

To everyone that lives to dream and create,
this book is for you.

Published by Running Press,
A Member of the Perseus Books Group

Books published by Running Press are available at special discounts for bulk purchases in the United States
by corporations, institutions, and other organizations. For more information, please contact the
Special Markets Department at the Perseus Books Group, 2300 Chestnut Street, Suite 200,
Philadelphia, PA 19103, or call (800) 810-4145, ext. 5000, or e-mail special.markets@perseusbooks.com.

ISBN 978-0-7624-4689-6
Library of Congress Control Number: 2012944542

E-book ISBN 978-0-7624-4825-8

9 8 7 6 5 4 3 2 1
Digit on the right indicates the number of this printing

Cover design by Corinda Cook
Interior design by Melissa Gerber
Edited by Jordana Tusman
Typography: Whitney, LaurenScript, Century Gothic Regular,
Katerino, and ITC Franklin Gothic Demi

Running Press Book Publishers
2300 Chestnut Street
Philadelphia, PA 19103-4371

Visit us on the web!
www.runningpress.com

Contents

Chapter 3
NECKLACES...........................64

Chapter 4
BRACELETS............................. 102

Chapter 5
EARRINGS 126

Chapter 6
RINGS................................. 156

• INTRODUCTION •

Sparkle Is a State of Mind!

Take everything your imagination conjures up when you hear the word *sparkle*—and throw it out the window. For me, *sparkle* has always had a different and very special meaning. Sparkle is a state of mind. Sparkle is a way of life. Sparkle is something I subscribed to many years ago when I set out on a journey to follow my dreams as a designer of fashion jewelry and accessories. Living the sparkling life is about making the most of what you have, wherever you are, right now. It's also about finding the beauty and inspiration in everything, even when it isn't so obvious. But mostly, it's about living with passion, creativity, and curiosity, and always following your dreams.

Fans near and far have asked me for advice about how to follow their dreams and make them a reality. I may not be the authority, but chasing dreams is organic for me. That's how I built my business and how I make my living. It's what motivates me and gets me through tough times. I believe that we all have the ability to follow our own dreams directly into the sparkling life that we want to lead.

The way I do it is to surround myself with inspiration, to always try to be optimistic (look on the sparkling side!), and to be as creative as I can every day. My hope with this book is that you will also feel that "spark" of inspiration, get some pearls of wisdom, and give yourself permission to step outside your comfort zone and try something new. Not only will you be

creating the pieces in this book and wearing them, too, but you'll also be making them your own.

Because jewelry is such a huge part of my world, I think it is the best place to start. Jewelry and personal adornment are emblematic of this life: colorful, unique, sometimes loud, at other times subtle, but always making a statement and telling the story of who you are. Now, let me take you on a journey into a world that I am very passionate about: jewelry and accessories.

• CHAPTER 1 •

History

Childhood

My love affair with self-adornment began when I was just a little girl. As the only child of young, artistic parents growing up in a bohemian southern California beach town, I guess I had it in my DNA. My mom was studying to be a painter and had a tiny art studio off our kitchen where we would paint and make crafts. My dad loved woodworking, photography, and collecting antique bottles in all colors, shapes, and sizes. Making art with my parents is one of my favorite memories. They had wonderful, eclectic taste, and our house was always a mixture of antique and modern.

My grandparents lived nearby and loved to travel. They toured exotic places like Japan, Russia, Istanbul, Morocco, London, and more, always bringing back delightful gifts and trinkets

from far-off lands. My very stylish grandmother had a beautiful closet where I would spend endless hours playing in her jewelry boxes, trying things on, and piling on her bangles, shoes, and hats. This is where I learned that the tiniest detail—a hand-carved wood button shaped like a bird, a filigree slide closure on an ivory bracelet, or the bow on the buckle of a platform shoe—could completely transform the simplest of pieces.

My creativity exploded around the age of five when I made my first jewelry pieces. My mother bought me some colorful blocks of bakeable polymer clay, and I immediately made elephant and rainbow pins, some beads, and a ring. I remember wearing these pieces so proudly—it was my first jewelry collection. Jewelry making was always my thing, even through years of ballet, horse shows, and piano lessons. In high school, I made collage pins out of vintage toys, watch parts, and seashells.

Beginnings in Fashion and Design

After graduating from high school, I had an opportunity to go to Europe and work as a fashion model. I ended up traveling back and forth between Barcelona, Paris, Munich, Belgium, Copenhagen, and more over the next three years. This was such an inspiring time in my life, being in the epicenter of the fashion world, traveling and working with top designers, photographers, and stylists. But I was never creatively fulfilled in front of the camera, so I began making jewelry again.

At a flea market in Paris, I found some old broken jewelry that reminded me of my childhood when I would take apart hand-me-down jewelry my grandma gave me. Feeling inspired, I picked up some polymer clay and jewelry tools on my way home. That night, I set up my design table on a folding tray in my studio apartment and started to create one-of-a-kind jewelry pieces that I had been thinking about. I made big clay crystal rings, long necklaces with flower-covered crosses, and beads and earrings that looked like gumballs. Pretty soon, stylists, photographers, and makeup artists started asking about my pieces and would often borrow them for shoots or fashion shows.

Meeting Alfonso and Starting the Business

Bitten by the creative bug, I decided to return home to Los Angeles to continue making jewelry while also pursuing my second passion and career as a makeup artist. It was right around this time that I met my artistic soulmate and future husband, Alfonso Campos, and my necklace played a special role in this serendipitous moment. The first words out of his mouth were, "Where did you get that necklace?!"

At first he didn't believe me when I told him that I had made it, so I was annoyed. I told him that it was more of a hobby and that I was really a makeup artist. He said, "I have never seen jewelry like that. If you can make that you should be a famous designer!"

I thought he was either the biggest charmer I had ever met or full of baloney! But as we talked late into the night, I discovered that he was also an artist and that we had many things in common including our love of fashion, foreign cinema, and obscure electronic music.

We started dating, and four years later, Tarina Tarantino Designs was born in our tiny apartment in West Hollywood, with nothing more than a lot of ambition and passion for what we were doing. That's not to say it was easy; it definitely wasn't. We had to keep our day jobs for the first few years, so it was like having two jobs, and it seemed as though we never slept.

When our collections debuted in 1995, minimalism was at its height. The backlash to the opulent 1980s had left girls like me hungry for some fashion inspiration. Buyers were not ready to showcase jewelry that had its own personality, and there were plenty of times when doors were closed in our faces.

Once Alfonso took our collection to a popular jewelry store on Melrose. They carried lots of interesting art jewelry and accessories, so I thought my pieces would be a perfect fit there. The owner stared at the collection and said, "Color? Big crystals? This chunky stuff? No way, it won't sell! Sorry, bye-bye!" Alfonso said, "You'll be calling me" as he walked out the door. I was crushed; I figured that if this store owner didn't like it, none of the other stores would.

I continued working at my retail cosmetics job and freelancing as a makeup artist; I was beginning to think that jewelry might never be anything but a hobby. But Alfonso used his experience at that shop to fuel his fire, and a few weeks later, he decided to shoot straight to the top. He called up the most difficult buyer to get an appointment with at Fred Segal. I told him he was crazy, that she bought only designer jewelry. He looked at me and said, "This is designer jewelry and you are the designer! And she is going to love it, I promise." How could I argue with that?

A week later, Alfonso had the appointment—and came home that very same day with a $5,000 order! The buyer said that this was exactly the kind of jewelry she had been looking for, with big stones and lots of color. She even showed him where she was going to merchandise it so we could make some special display pieces. I couldn't believe it! My jewelry was going to sit on the shelf at one of the most important stores in Los Angeles next to the most notable designers!

The first day my jewelry was on sale at Fred Segal, Claire Danes and Drew Barrymore stopped by on a shopping trip and bought everything. The next week, Claire was on the red carpet wearing it to a movie premiere. Oh, and that buyer who called my jewelry "chunky stuff"? He did end up calling. But it was too late; we were already selling to his competitor down the street. Vindication was never more satisfying than when I told him that Fred Segal had the exclusive now and was selling lots of those chunky rings!

It was around this time that I decided to cut my long, curly hair boy-short. When I was growing it out, I started making bejeweled hair clips to keep it in place. I called them "hair jewelry." As soon as I wore these glittering clips, women were stopping me and asking where I got them. One of those women was actress Ashley Judd, who bought them right off of me, literally, and wore them to a Golden Globe party that night. After that, she called and requested custom pieces to go with her entire wardrobe.

As my hair accessories caught fire, I was approached by jewelry boutique owner, Jennifer Kaufman, who catered to the biggest stars in Hollywood. She tracked me down and said, "I was told you are the girl behind this gorgeous jewelry. I would love to carry it in my store." She devoted an entire case to our collections and was an early supporter of our burgeoning brand.

Before we knew it, we were getting calls from all the important fashion magazines like *Vogue*, *Bazaar*, *Glamour*, and *Elle*, requesting samples from our collections to feature in their editorial pages. In 1998, *People* magazine contacted us to do a profile story on our company, and how our pieces started the hair jewelry trend. Later that year, Oprah invited us to appear on her show about young entrepreneurs. Two years later, our wedding would be featured in *InStyle* magazine. It was a whirlwind that felt like a fairy-tale come to life and launched our little company into the fashion stratosphere.

The Road to The Sparkle Factory

I t had always been a dream of mine to have my own business, and as our brand grew over the years, that dream got bigger and bigger. What started in the dining room of our tiny apartment had now taken over every room. The hallway was lined with shipping boxes, the living room was the showroom where we met with stylists, and the dining room was for design and production. I would design and make the jewelry, and Alfonso would do everything else from sales, marketing, and press to painting tiny flowerpots and sanding rings. We realized we needed help when we were falling behind on orders, so we hired our first employee, who was eventually joined by seven others.

It got very cramped in the apartment and that was making us less productive, so we decided to take the next step and moved the business into a little studio in West Hollywood. We discovered that the studio had once been the dressing room for the famous silent film actor and director Fatty Arbuckle, and had also been frequented by many other silent film stars. We loved the history but the space was a disaster, so after hours at night, Alfonso gutted it, installed display cases he had built, and painted the walls in shimmering ice cream colors. We turned it into a jewel box studio that was visited by stylists and stars.

On a given day, I would be meeting in the studio with celebrities like Cyndi Lauper or shipping pieces to Madonna's stylist. Everyone who visited fell in love with the charming atmosphere, the cool music, and the cases full of glittering jewelry. We even bejeweled the numbers on the door to our unit and painted it pink. I still have that door!

After 9/11, we, like many other businesses, went through some very tough times and had to downsize, but we held on and our business survived thanks to our perseverance and many loyal customers. In 2002, everything changed for us when Cameron Diaz wore my turquoise Lucite carved rose bracelet on the red carpet at the Oscars. She layered it with an armful of diamond bangles, which made it stand out even more dramatically. Suddenly we were overwhelmed with orders, had to hire more people, and realized it was time to move again. This time we headed to downtown L.A. and the fashion district.

We found the perfect loft space for our design offices and opened our showroom across the street, but the vision of having our own factory never went away. We eventually needed more space to create and manufacture our collections right in Los Angeles. The Sparkle Factory became that special space. Today, it is where we create everything from our sparkling jewelry and accessory collections to cosmetics, home collections, and more.

The Sparkle Factory is a place to dream and create. It is where we make special pieces for glittering stars such as Katy Perry, Dakota Fanning, Emma Stone, Kelly Osbourne, Nicki Minaj, and Mindy Kaling. It is a place where big ideas are encouraged and the importance of the tiniest detail is understood. It is all about the blood, sweat, and sparkle that go into those details. It is my design lab, and every member of my sparkling team knows that each day here will be different, because there is always an exciting new collection to create or another project to conquer. We are also especially proud of making our pieces right here in the U.S.A., keeping it local, supporting jobs, and promoting American-made fashion.

The Boutiques

MILAN

In 2002, we opened our very first shop-in-shop at the Fiorucci Emporium in Milan, Italy. As it happened, the legendary Italian designer Elio Fiorucci had seen our collections while our Italian partner Sofia Castelli was showing them to another buyer. He loved the pieces so much that he invited us to open a corner in his shop on the spot. Elio must have known something we didn't, because our brand quickly caught on with Italian fashionistas, editors, and starlets alike. Later that year, we were credited with helping to create a new trend in Italian fashion known as "Kidult" along with Prada and Dolce & Gabbana. Several years later, we opened our

own freestanding boutique in the center of the historic fashion capital just steps away from the Duomo, which continues to be visited by an international clientele that describes the store as a "sparkling jewel box."

LOS ANGELES

In 2005, our flagship store debuted on Melrose Avenue in Los Angeles. Another dream had come true for a girl who spent her teenage years begging her parents to drive her to L.A. just to shop on this street. With the opening of our L.A. store, we gave customers and fans everywhere access to current and classic collections along with special merchandise available only in this location.

NEW YORK

In 2007, while walking the streets of SoHo, Manhattan, we saw a man putting up a "for lease" sign on a tiny storefront, on Greene Street right across from Louis Vuitton. We turned it into a gem of a store. Unfortunately, the building was purchased five years later by a shoe brand that opted to build their own flagship store. We're hoping to find another New York location very soon.

· ·

Sitting down to write this book has given me a rare opportunity to go back and revisit the journey I have been on. While there have been many fairy-tale moments like our romantic and glittering wedding,

having two delightful daughters, seeing my jewelry on the cover of a magazine—oh, and being made into a Mattel Barbie Doll was definitely a "pinch me" moment!—there have also been many challenges and roadblocks to navigate along the road to The Sparkle Factory. But each of these challenges, just like the successes, has taught us the many valuable lessons that we use each and every day to continue to build our brand.

I truly hope that this book will inspire you to express yourself through jewelry design and to create the treasures and keepsakes that tell your story to be passed down for generations to come.

Now, I want to invite you into the magical place that I call the Sparkle Factory.

Jarina

CHAPTER 2

Design and Inspiration

Freeing Your Inner Designer

So you want to design some jewelry but don't know where to start? Maybe you don't think you can be a designer or that you don't have a creative bone in your body. Well, guess what? You do! We are creative beings by nature; we are programmed to make things and have done so for thousands of years. All you have to do is allow yourself to free your inner designer and educate yourself on whatever you are passionate about. If that passion happens to be fashion and jewelry design, then devour every book you can find on these subjects.

"Be inspired, but be original."

When I was working as a fashion model and living in Europe, I would read book after book on train rides from Paris to Belgium and during afternoon siestas in Spain. I would visit every museum, especially ones that had a fashion or jewelry exhibit. I paid special attention to the things that really attracted me, like Art Nouveau and Mid-Century modernism. Some of my favorite books are biographies on great designers like Elsa Schiaparelli, Barbara Hulanicki of Biba, and Coco Chanel. These fascinating and inspiring women paved the way for generations of designers.

Inspiration

Inspiration: what is it? Where does it come from? When this question was put to the creative genius Charlie Chaplin, he answered quite simply and brilliantly, "From the whole pageantry of life." Sparks of inspiration are like butterflies; they can come from anywhere and everywhere, but you must always have your net ready. If you want to be more creative you should always surround yourself with as much inspiration as possible; seek it out, and always be ready with your notebook or camera.

The challenge comes with capturing the inspiration and helping it make its way from your imagination into reality. Creativity and inspiration can sometimes be elusive, mystifying, and intangible. These are the times when you must do something to shake it loose and get it flowing again.

CREATE YOUR OWN RESOURCE LIBRARY: I have hundreds of books on every subject that interests me including art, design, architecture, fashion, history, culture, travel, and on and on. When I discover something new, I immediately find a book about it, so my library is always growing. Think about all the things that interest you, and collect new and vintage books on these subjects. You can also get inspired from old storybooks. Luckily my mom kept most of my childhood books from *Alice in Wonderland* to *The Wonderful Wizard of Oz*, both of which have inspired my work. Make yourself a little library or research space, even if it's just a corner. A place that is just for reading encourages more reading.

CREATE AN "INSPIRATIONARIUM": This is a shelf in my design lab where I showcase all the curiosities that I collect to inspire me: toys, trinkets, artifacts, and treasures. I really encourage collecting anything and everything that you love. Pay attention to the colors, shapes, and stories behind these objects. Sometimes one simple object can ignite an idea for an entire collection.

USE YOUR IMAGINATION AND MEMORY: You are probably thinking this is pretty obvious, but sometimes we forget to use the most powerful and magical tool we possess. In our mysterious and wonderful minds, we can create whatever we want, go to different places, and

dream up worlds that do not exist. We can also go back in time and remember the things that we loved in our childhood, and use those things to inspire us now. Recycling these memories into our work lets them out into the open to be shared with others.

JOT IT DOWN: I always carry little Moleskine notebooks with me, the kind without any lines, just blank pages. I love them because I can sketch ideas and make notes next to it. You may not know the outcome or what these little notes can become, but that's just part of the process. I have a basket that I keep all my sketchbooks in, and when I need some inspiration, I just start flipping through them—it's like digging for treasure.

MAKE STORYBOARDS: Storyboards, also called mood boards, are a great way to collect all your ideas, sketches, materials, and photo inspirations in one place. Here at the factory, we take an "everything but the kitchen sink" approach to storyboarding. Nothing is off limits if it's something that you like; if you can stick a pin through it, put it on your storyboard! My storyboards are always crafted to look like an art collage; they are dimensional and tactile like the one you see here from our Tilt-a-Whirl vintage carnival and circus-themed collection. Some unusual things you can collect for your boards are vintage stickers, postcards, flags, ribbons, beads, chain, and more. You can also make virtual storyboards on websites like Pinterest, Image Spark, or the Moodboard app for the iPad.

LISTEN TO MUSIC, RELAX, AND HAVE FUN: Music is an integral part of my design process. I cannot work without it; it helps to get me in the creative mood and keeps me focused. I like to make playlists around my collections or stream my own curated radio stations online. Different genres of music can also inspire design. My Strange Delight collection was inspired partly by a Roxy Music song called "No Strange Delight." Music will help you relax and let your mind go, and this is when the best work happens.

GET OUT AND GET CURIOUS: Grab your notebook and camera and take a walk around your neighborhood; visit a museum or gallery or a place you have never been, but always wanted to go. Living in Los Angeles, I love to take advantage of all the cultural centers that it has to offer. For my Sugar Skull collections, I visit the historical Olvera Street for ideas. The shops are overflowing with eye-popping, colorful Mexican artifacts, trinkets, and clothing. Think about places in your town, no matter how large or small, that you are curious about and go check them out. I promise that you will come home with lots of new influences.

READ FASHION MAGAZINES AND BLOGS: Knowing what is "on trend" does not mean you are following trends. Looking at great fashion magazines and blogs just makes you want to have more fun with your design work and wardrobe. Keeping up with the world of fashion and design also makes your work better and more relevant.

HAVE COFFEE WITH YOUR GRANDMA!

My absolute favorite way to get inspired is by sitting down with my grandma and asking her all about the things she has seen, places she has gone, and her favorite memories from the past. The last time I sat down with her, she told me all about her dazzling

trip to Hong Kong in 1978. You can do this with any member of your family, a friend, or mentor. They may tell you about something they saw or did that you have never heard of. They may even have photos from these places or moments in time that you can use on your mood boards. When inspirations come from real places, they have deeper meanings. And you can celebrate the life of one of your favorite relatives with a piece of jewelry that you design. **CHALLENGE YOURSELF:** If you like to work with wire and beads, try sculpting pieces with clay. If you only make things that are abstract, try incorporating faces into your pieces, or small figures of whatever motivates you. Challenging yourself to try new things, work with new materials, or design something differently is the best way to grow as an artist and hone your skills.

Materials and Sourcing

When making anything, often the biggest challenge is finding the exact materials that you need to make your ideas come to life. Today I am able to have many of the beads, cameos, and charms for my collections made exclusively, but it was not always this way. I realized early on that much of the creativity comes in the improvisation of materials.

I dreamed of having beautiful custom beads made from Lucite, glass, and wood, but in the beginning I couldn't afford the high minimums to have these components produced, so I found materials like polymer clay to make my beads and pendants. I loved the way this material could simulate marbleized resin beads and millefiori. This clay also gave me the freedom to create anything and everything I dreamt up. I used vintage buttons to give my pieces a Bakelite look and feel. I took apart old costume jewelry and would press the stones into my clay cocktail rings. I used sequins, paillettes, and even glitter confetti to add extra sparkle inexpensively.

I hope that after reading this book you will never look at sourcing materials the same way again. From now on, everywhere you go, you should always be on the lookout for anything that you can use to create jewelry masterpieces. I always have my designer radar tuned in no matter where I am.

I'm not just talking about while you are strolling down the aisles of your local craft or bead store. I'm talking about looking for materials in the most unexpected places: the 99-cent store, the toy store, the flea market, the supermarket, eBay, the hardware store, the back of your closet, the attic, the basement, your child's toy box! Everything you need to create beautiful

"Getting creative with the materials you choose for your projects will make your pieces more interesting and distinctive."

jewelry is all around you, everywhere you go—and you don't have to spend a lot of money! The materials I used in these projects were mostly sourced from local suppliers and places like the ones mentioned previously. The projects are meant to inspire you, and your pieces should not necessarily look exactly the same as what you see in this book unless you want them to.

Finding materials these days is so much easier than when I started years ago. With the Internet the sky is the limit, and when you wake up in the middle of the night thinking about star-shaped sequins or mini top hats, chances are you will be able to find exactly what you are looking for. If you can't find what you want for your pieces, stop and think about how you can make what you need, or go out and hunt for things that might be used to improvise the things you want, like the plastic baby barrettes used for the Sweet Shop Earrings (page 143).

Getting creative about the materials you use is what will ultimately make your pieces more distinctive. If you can't find the bead that you want, consider drilling holes through small objects that could become beads. Don't have enough chain to make your necklace? Link different chains together to create a more interesting chain. Can't find a base for your pendant? Repurpose an oversized earring into a pendant, as I did in the Cinnamon Girl Bib

Necklace (page 77). Quite often, the things we need are around us or can be replaced with other things if we are open to the possibilities.

Find a list of some of my favorite resources on pages 263 to 265. They're there to help you find materials and tools for some of the projects in this book.

MATERIALS

The following is a list of materials that you will be using for some of the projects to help bring your jewelry and accessories to life.

BEADS: Over the years I have collected or had custom made the thousands and thousands of different styles that line the shelves, walls, and pretty much every nook and cranny around the factory. The thing I love most about beads is the versatility and all the different ways you can use them in your work. In the Cinnamon Girl Bib Necklace (page 77), you will see that beads don't always have to live on a string; they can be used to embellish as well.

CABOCHONS: Traditionally, cabochons or "cabs" are rounded, polished gemstones. In the modern jewelry world, cabochon also refers to pretty much any smallish flatback object used for embellishment.

CHAIN: Picking the right chain is very important, because this is what links everything together. Having chain available in different sizes and colors will give your design work variety. There are thousands of different types of chain from metal to plastic. If there are certain types of chain that you particularly like, try to use them in the jewelry you create. Different types of chain lie differently on the body, so it is important to choose the correct type for each project.

"Choose chain for your projects with a smooth finish and no rough edges. Using a higher quality chain will make your pieces more comfortable and durable."

FINDINGS: Findings are the worker bees of jewelry making. They include jump rings, head pins, lobster clasps, ear hooks, and a variety of metal settings and parts used to construct your jewelry pieces. It's important to stock different gauges and sizes so you always have the correct ones on hand. At the Sparkle Factory, we have hundreds of different sizes, but you need only a few of each to cover the bases of jewelry making. A great rule of thumb when it comes to jump rings, head pins, and eye pins is always to use the thickest gauge possible. The more substantial your findings are, the more expensive your pieces will look and feel. As a Sparkle Factory rule, I always make sure my jump rings "kiss" and align perfectly. This reinforces their strength and will help guarantee the integrity of the finished piece.

Treasure Box

Keep a treasure box filled with toys, odd buttons, broken jewelry, little trinkets, and items found in nature—just throw in anything that can be used for later projects. Look for things you might normally dismiss; you will find that these old and seemingly useless things can really inspire.

This is my little treasure box that was originally given to me by my great grandma Matilda. Inside, I have all kinds of nostalgic things from my childhood, travels, and adventures. The collection of random things makes it easy and fun to discover little ideas to incorporate into my design work.

FLATBACK CRYSTALS: When it comes to great jewelry, crystals are the icing on the cake. Used correctly, they add sparkling effects that make your designs look luxurious and irresistible. Used incorrectly, they can make your piece look less desirable. The finest crystal in the world is Swarovski, which is what I prefer to use in my jewelry collections. I suggest you use this gorgeous crystal whenever you can. Even if you sprinkle just a few of them on a piece, they give a magical shine that makes anything look prettier and brings your creations to life.

TRIM: This includes ribbon, cord, leather, fabric flowers, bows, rosettes, and so on. These are not traditional materials for jewelry design, but that's exactly why I like them. They give your pieces interesting texture and shape. Using different types of trim is a great way to add color or help tell the story of your design.

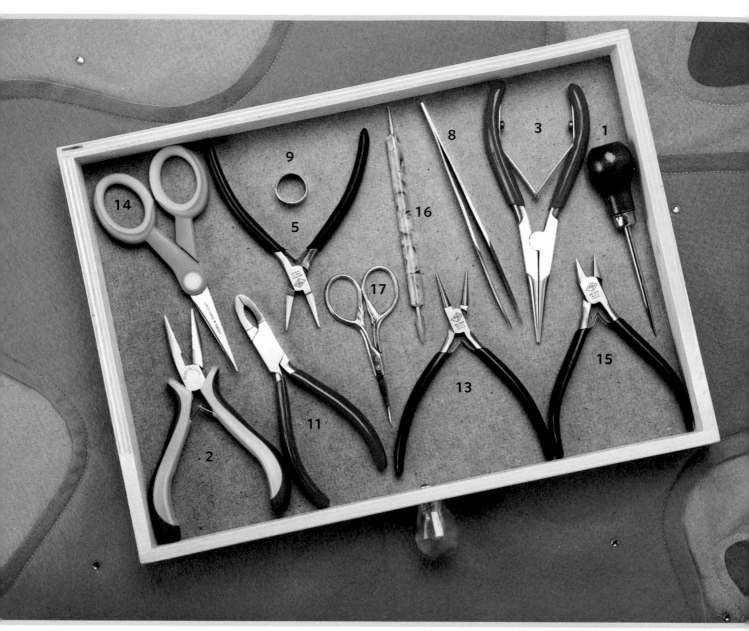

TOOLS

These are the essential tools you will need to complete the projects in this book. You can store them in a canvas tool pouch (or an ordinary jewelry roll). Pliers can be stored on a wooden plier stand. The most important thing is to always use the proper tool for the job. This will make your tools last longer and ensure better craftsmanship in your design work.

1. **AWL:** Clears debris from bead channels, picks away excess glue, helps tie knots, and arranges chain in straight lines.

2. **CHAIN-NOSE PLIERS:** Multipurpose pliers for your jewelry tool kit. I use these to bend wire, pull beading cord, close jump rings and chain links, and more. I prefer the serrated version as they have a better grip.

3. **CHAIN-OPENING PLIERS:** Also known as bow-opening pliers, chain-opening pliers are used to open chain and attach chain links.

4. **CRIMPING PLIERS:** Learning to crimp properly is essential in jewelry making. I use this specialized tool to close my crimp beads securely. It folds the crimp bead around itself, providing the strongest crimp and ensuring the integrity of your finished piece.

5. **FLAT-NOSE PLIERS:** Stabilizes jump rings when you open or close them with the jump ring tool.

6. **ALLIGATOR AND FOLDER CLIPS:** Holds and clamps pieces while they dry. I also use them to keep beads from escaping by clamping them to the end of the cord when I'm making necklaces and bracelets.

7. **DISPOSABLE BAKING PANS:** I like to use these for everything: to dry glued pieces, to catch hot glue drips, to bake polymer clay projects, to hold beads, and more.

8. **JEWELRY TWEEZERS:** For placing stones.

9. **JUMP RING TOOL:** Also known as a jump ring-closing tool or a jump ring opener, this tool fits on your finger like a ring and makes opening and closing heavy gauge jump rings a breeze. Just slide the jump ring into one of the channels and open or close gently with pliers.

10. **LARGE CUTTER PLIERS:** Cuts all varieties of craft wire including heavy gauges, beading cords, bulk chains, and soft metal findings.

11. **LOOP-CLOSING PLIERS:** Makes your jump rings "kiss" tightly together after closing them.

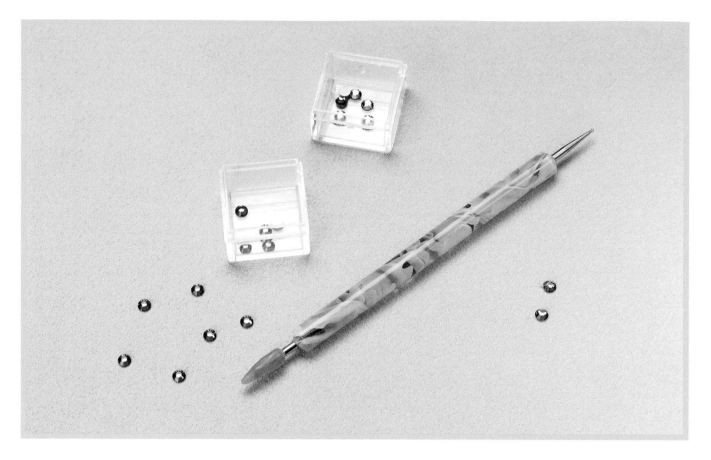

12. **MEMORY WIRE SHEARS:** Cuts memory wire. Memory wire has a special tension and strength that can ruin regular cutters.

13. **ROUND-NOSE PLIERS:** Creates loops on head pins, eye pins, and wire.

14. **SCISSORS:** Cuts thread, jelly cord, leather cord, and most jewelry stringing materials.

15. **SMALL CUTTER PLIERS:** Helps you get into tighter spaces and nip away excess beading cord, jelly cord, or smaller, softer craft wire.

16. **THE SPARKLE FACTORY MAGIC WAND (PAGE 265):** This amazing little tool is used to pick up flatback crystals, cabochons, sequins, and more. To make one yourself, you can use a chopstick, orange stick, pencil, or nail art tool like I used here. Simply add a bit of jeweler's wax to the tip, shape into a point, and your Magic Wand is ready. Always pick up the stones gently and put them delicately into place; pressing too hard will leave wax residue on the stones.

17. **THREAD SCISSORS:** Cuts delicate thread.

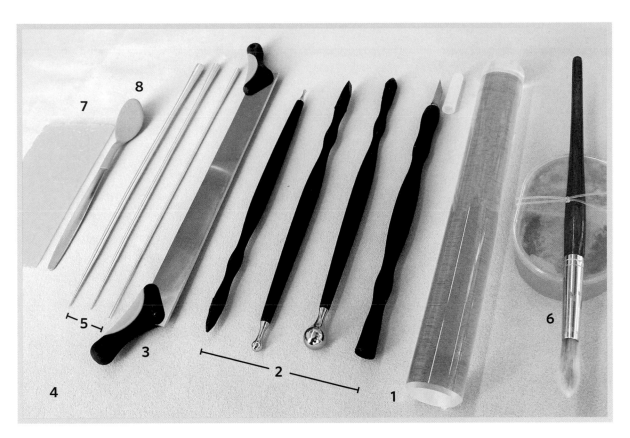

POLYMER CLAY TOOLS AND MATERIALS

1. **ACRYLIC CLAY ROLLER:** Rolls out clay in even, smooth sheets.

2. **ASSORTED CLAY SHAPING AND MANIPULATION TOOLS (INCLUDING CLAY DETAILING TOOLS):** Shapes, cuts, and creates patterns in clay.

3. **CLAY CUTTING BLADE:** Slices polymer clay logs, snakes, and canes.

4. **CLAY MAT:** A non-skid silicone mat is used to protect surfaces when working with clay. This mat can also be used to bake your clay creations.

5. **CLAY SKEWERS:** Long, skinny metal rods used to make holes or tunnels in beads and clay pieces.

6. **CORNSTARCH/BRUSH:** Use cornstarch in push molds for better clay release. Brush cornstarch on the mold using a soft paintbrush before each use.

7. **SCULPEY TEXTURE MAKER:** The texture maker is for pressing into clay to create textual surfaces, like for the lace pattern in Acid Cameo Western Belt Buckle (page 223).

8. **SILICONE BABY SPOON:** A great shaping/smoothing tool for getting rid of finger-prints in the clay or pressing in large crystals and stones.

ADHESIVES

GLUE: Today's adhesives come in many varieties; it seems as though there is a glue for almost every application. Because navigating the different kinds available can be overwhelming, I use only three simple adhesives in this book, and honestly, unless you are opening a factory like mine, this is all you need.

HOT GLUE GUN: You may already have one, and it doesn't need to be fancy. However, if you get one with a slim nozzle it will make jewelry work easier. Hot glue is pretty forgiving, and in fact, if you mess up and get it in the wrong spot, most times you can let it dry and peel it away and start over.

PERMABOND: This glue has a gel-like texture and superior strength. It's great for attaching metal to plastic. It has an immediate bond and a quick dry time. I use it for things like attaching earring posts to beads or cabochons.

E6000: This is the workhorse all-purpose glue for almost any project. It dries more slowly than hot glue and gives you more time to move embellishments around. I like to transfer E6000 into a needle-tip squeeze bottle. This will help minimize the fumes and give you precise control. When using any adhesives, always make sure to have proper ventilation in your workspace.

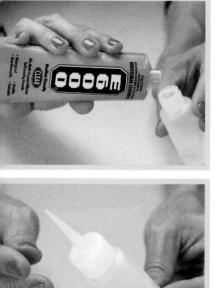

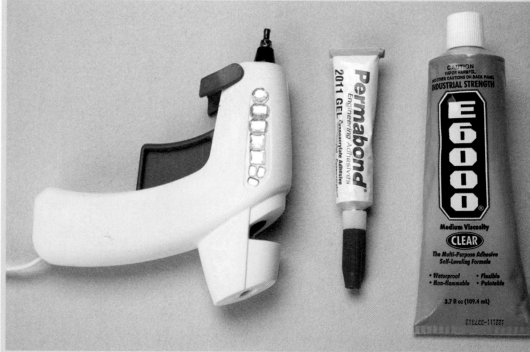

Organizing Your Workspace

Being organized is a great time-saver and keeps us relaxed and focused when working on projects. The problem is that we are human and pretty messy by nature, myself included. Try as I will, I still manage to create lots of chaos at my design table, but I accept it as just part of my process. We have literally hundreds of thousands of different components and beads here at the factory. Keeping all these tiny parts "wrangled" is a big job, and we have come up with some clever ways to store our materials over the years.

Use clear containers to store your beads, findings, and assorted materials. The most important thing for me is to be able to see my beads easily and not have to hunt for them for hours. I place the containers on shelves, grouping them by color. At the factory, I use clear acrylic boxes or bottles to store my beads, but in my home studio, I like to use repurposed glass jam jars. Repurposing peanut butter or jam jars for bead storage is easy. Just soak the label off and spray paint the lids to make them look cute.

Techniques

ATTACHING CLASPS:

1. The most important thing is to first choose a good clasp. I prefer the lobster variety for the most secure and comfortable closure.

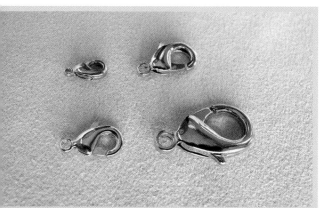

2. First, attach the lobster clasp to a jump ring and attach the jump ring to one side of the necklace or bracelet using a crimp bead.

3. On the other end of the piece, attach a jump ring or seamless ring for your clasp to attach to. Use a crimp bead to finish this side of your piece as well.

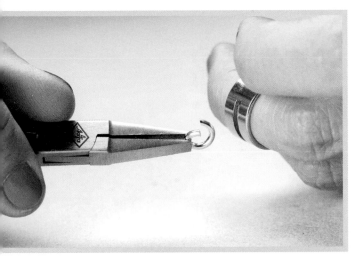

JUMP RINGS:

1. To open and close jump rings properly, use flat-nose or chain-nose pliers and a jump ring tool.

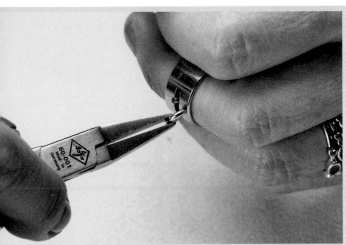

2. Insert the jump ring into the tool and push forward at the split. Attach the jump ring into place and close with the jump ring tool. Finally, use the loop-closing pliers to make the jump rings secure and "kiss" them together tightly.

CRIMPING:

1. Thread cable through the crimp bead and through the clasp. Then pass the cable back through the crimp bead and leave a 3½ inch to 4½ inch tail.

2. Use the back part of the crimping pliers (shaped like lips) to pinch the crimp bead into a "u," which will secure a wire on each side of the bend in the cable.

3. Move the bead to the front "rounder" part of the pliers' jaw (shaped like a lemon). Gently press together and "fold" the crimp bead into a rounded secure shape. Trim excess wire with small cutter pliers.

CONNECTING CHAIN:

1. Using the chain-opening pliers (also called bow-opening pliers), slide the chain link onto the nose of the pliers.

2. Press open firmly.

3. Slip into the first link of the chain you are connecting to.

4. Using chain-nose pliers, press firmly together to close the link.

LOOPING EYE PINS AND HEAD PINS:

1. Start by threading the bead onto the head pin or eye pin. Cut excess length if necessary. You need to leave about ¼ to ½ inch of wire to make a loop, depending on how large you need it to be.

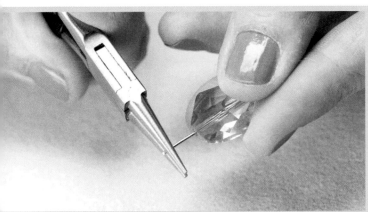

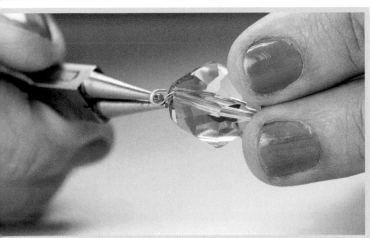

2. Using round-nose pliers, grab the tip of the pin and roll toward the bead.

3. Bend the neck of the loop back slightly to create the perfect loop. Using chain-nose pliers, gently close the loop until it "kisses" together.

KNOTTING "STRETCH MAGIC" JELLY CORD: When using clear cord like Stretch Magic for necklaces or bracelets, you must first pre-stretch the cord. Do this by cutting the length you need (always leave yourself at least 3 inches for easy handling) and stretching it. This prevents the piece from stretching out later. To finish a piece, take the ends of the cord and tie together with a minimum of four knots, one on top of the other. The larger or heavier the project is, the more knots you will need to secure it; sometimes you will need up to eight knots. Once you have finished the knots, trim any excess and tuck into the nearest bead hole with a micro pearl drop of E6000 glue. This will hide the ugly knot, make the piece look polished, and add extra security to the knotted ends. A final tip is to use a bead with a large hole to hide the knot easily.

HAND SEWING: Using sewing techniques in jewelry and hair accessories may seem unlikely, but I find myself turning to my needle and thread more and more often. What I love—especially on something like a headband—is that sewing your pieces together makes them more flexible and comfortable when worn. What you need is pretty basic: a needle, thread, and thimble. The stitch styles I like to use are very simple: use a running stitch for gathering or creating ruffles; use an overcast stitch for seaming two ends of ribbon or fabric together; and use a securing stitch for adding embellishments, sequins, crystals, buttons, and more to pieces.

MAKING AND USING POLYMER PUSH MOLDS:

To make the mold:

1. Using Sculpey Super Elasticlay Moldmaker, take about 2½ times the size of the object (cameo, bead, button, etc.) you are molding and condition it until soft.

2. Brush the object with cornstarch to avoid sticking.

3. Press the object into the clay firmly and evenly.

4. Gently remove the object and bake the clay mold in the oven as directed by the instructions on the package. You will be able to use this mold over and over to create embellishments for your clay designs.

Using a push mold:

1. Dust the mold cavity with cornstarch for easy release after baking. Condition a small amount of Sculpey polymer clay into a ball.

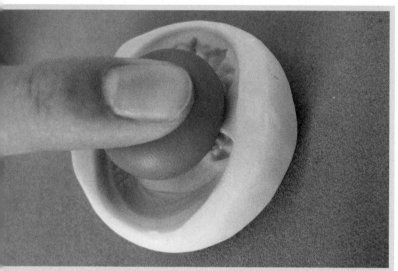

2. Press the conditioned ball of clay evenly into the mold.

3. Gently release to prevent distortion of the object.

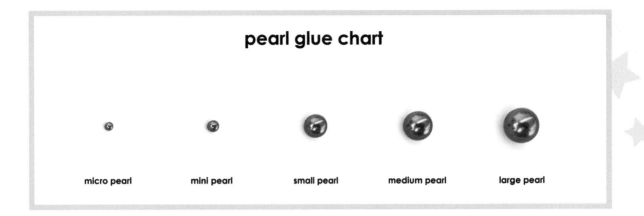

pearl glue chart

| micro pearl | mini pearl | small pearl | medium pearl | large pearl |

GLUING: It's very important to use just enough glue to get the job done, but never too much. Oozing glue makes for unattractive jewelry, and not enough glue can give you a "starved bond" and cause things to fall apart. What I try to do is look at the surfaces I want to bond together, and assess just how much I will need to cover only the surface areas. There is an art to proper gluing, and practice makes perfect. To help you with the process, throughout the book I have suggested the sizes of glue dots or "pearls" that I want you to use. Follow the chart above so you know exactly what size I am referring to in each project.

Be sure to give your projects enough time to dry before wearing them. I would suggest 12 to 24 hours minimum, depending on the climate you are working in. Your pieces will dry slower in cold weather and faster in warm weather.

"The best thing about making your own jewelry is that you can customize the fit. Just like clothing, jewelry always looks better when it's tailored to fit you perfectly."

Design Process

TELLING A STORY: How does jewelry tell a story? It can be a story from childhood or one that you dream up. For my Wonderful Wizard of Oz collections, I wanted to showcase the part in the movie that goes from black-and-white into color, so I illustrated Dorothy and the witches in full color against a black-and-white background. To tell stories on a micro level, you have to work out the details so they make sense and support the overall theme of the design.

SYMBOLISM: Using symbolic shapes and motifs will help you convey the feeling and story through your pieces. As examples, I often use symbols like skulls, hearts, stars, and flowers to represent different feelings. The shapes should also add to the story. For instance, a teardrop shape gives an emotional or dramatic flair to a piece, whereas circular shapes evoke a sense of calm and uniformity.

OPPOSING THEMES: One of my favorite ways to create interest in my design work is to juxtapose

opposites like light with dark, skulls with hearts, cute with subversive, and crystals with wood. My I Love You/I Hate You collections exemplify this design principle perfectly by mixing confectionary sweet pink with a dark message.

COLOR: Shocking pink; tangerine; acid lime; turquoise; milky white; and

siam red. I see the world through rainbow-colored glasses, and it's why I tinted my hair fuchsia years ago, the ultimate expression of my obsession with color. Choosing color combinations for my collections and creating complementary palettes is my favorite part of the design process. I get a rush from discovering unusual color partnerships, like olive green with lavender pink. It's like candy without the calories! Color can be nostalgic, emotional, arresting, and relaxing. It is a language all on its own. Choosing colors that work well together can be learned, but I prefer that you trust your instincts and go with what you love.

There are some great tricks for color composition. I like to play with objects or materials to get inspiration for colors. For example, I have tons of colored pencils; I collect them like mad. Why? Because playing with them and moving them around on a table can inspire new color combinations and ideas. This is when your "inspirationarium" will come in handy, playing with all those trinkets and knickknacks. Different objects paired together can encourage great color stories.

Now that you are inspired and know how to use the basic tools, we can sit down and start creating something together. In the following chapters, you will see projects that are influenced by some of my favorite pieces from my jewelry collections over the years.

Just remember to be inspired, but be original! Inspiration can come from something else, but it should always morph into something new. The way designers, artists, and everyone else for that matter find their ideas is as varied as there are stars in the sky. Nobody is exactly the same, and as an artist, I encourage you to always look for new ways to find inspiration too.

Kaliedescope
Fantastical

+ Painted Elephants K
+ Disney
+ Ballet Russe
+ Sugar cookies

Hair accessories:
• Headbands
• Bow clips
• Jeweled clips
• petit chapeau
• feather crowns
• feather clips

Jewelry
• pom pom earrings
• _____ Bracelets
_____ bracelets

SEQUIN & Chain

Layered
big Sequins,
METAL,
crystal bead
or Metal chain
fringe

"Grab a sketchbook and draw your ideas. Even doodles can become great inspirations for your jewelry designs."

CHAPTER 3

Necklaces

Tokyo Toy Store Matinee Necklace

This project is inspired by the Kidult fashion culture and my collaborations with such fantastic toy icons as Hello Kitty, Barbie, and designer toy pioneers Kidrobot. I gave Hello Kitty a new signature look with pink hair, was immortalized as a Barbie Doll, and created mini toy jewelry worlds with KidRobot. Toys are like little pieces of art and are endlessly inspiring. Collecting toys has been in my blood since my early days of model horse trading (I still have my collection!).

Inspirations

For this project, I simply got out my box of toys and charms and took a few things off the shelf in my office. What takes this jewelry piece from kid to couture is the way the materials (in this case, toys, charms, and erasers) are utilized on the necklace. The type of chain and the ironic use of toys create an irreverent couture necklace, one with a playful and avant-garde look.

materials:

(6-8) silver eye screw bails (.051 gauge)

3" large toy charm for focal pendant

(12-16) miscellaneous charms like toys, Japanese erasers, beads, etc.

(6-12) 2" silver head pins (.045 gauge)

26" total length chain (including charm spacers)

    (1) 8" cut length 5mm silver-plated chain

    (1) 2½" cut length 10mm blue aluminum chain

    (1) 2½" cut length 9mm black aluminum chain

    (2) 3½" cut length 8mm gold-plated chains

    (1) 3" cut length 6mm silver-plated chain

    (1) 3½" cut length 8mm silver-plated chain

    (1) 3" cut length 4mm silver-plated chain

(10-15) 6mm silver-plated jump rings (.045 gauge)

(1) 10mm silver-plated jump ring (.045 gauge)

tools:

Awl

Flat-nose pliers

E6000 glue

Round-nose pliers

Chain-nose pliers

Jump ring tool

process:

1. Use the flat-nose pliers to twist the screw eye finding into the top center of the focal toy pendant and any other smaller toys or erasers you want to use on the necklace. To insert a screw eye finding more easily, use an awl to make a small indentation in the charm, and then twist the screw eye into place. Keep twisting until the thread of the screw eye finding is no longer visible and fits snugly. Pull gently on the finding to make sure it is secure.

2. The ring on the screw eye finding should be facing forward. This will ensure that the focal toy pendant will hang properly on your necklace.

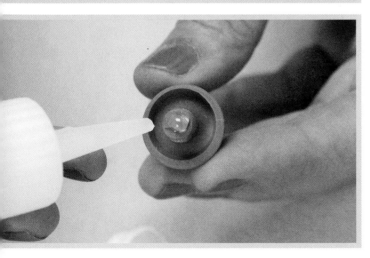

3. Since you are using cute erasers, you should make sure they are secure (many of these are segmented and can come apart). A small pearl-size drop of E6000 will bond pieces permanently together.

4. Create connector beads (to connect different pieces of chain together) using the flat-nose pliers to twist the screw eye findings into both the top and the bottom of the toy or eraser.

5. Make bead charms by sliding the beads onto a head pin and making a loop at the top with round-nose pliers. Remember to make the loops as pretty and round as possible. This helps the charms to hang nicely and looks more professional. Try stacking different sizes and colors of plastic beads together to make abstract-shaped charms.

6. Link the chains together by opening the last link with chain-nose pliers (or the chain-opening pliers) and connecting them in a random pattern. My chain here is about 26" long, but you should customize your length to what works for you.

7. Attach the connector beads to the lower part of the chain and add a thinner chain between them so that the toy pendant lies nicely.

8. Using chain-nose pliers and the jump ring tool, attach the toy pendant. Use the larger 10mm jump ring so the chain will flow through it nicely.

9. Using chain-nose pliers and the jump ring tool, add the additional charms in a random pattern, concentrating them on the lower half of the necklace. I like to put my necklace on a dress form at this time so I can attach the charms on the front of the chains so that they lie properly. If you don't have a dress form, hanging it from a hook will do the trick, too.

"At the factory we use a dress form as a way to see how necklaces will lay on the neck and body."

"My collaborations with icons like Hello Kitty, Barbie, and more have allowed me to create pieces that are nostalgic and playful for grown-up girls."

Cinnamon Girl Bib Necklace

When I was a little girl in the 1970s, my mom and I would make art in her tiny studio. With a Neil Young record playing in the background, we would create colorful psychedelic figures out of crepe paper and newspaper, little pins out of tiny vintage photographs, and paintings of horses and flowers—we even wallpapered our refrigerator one day! But my favorite art projects always involved beads, of course. We painted mason jars and covered them in beads, or made topiary bead trees at Christmastime. She taught me that beads are not just for stringing; just like any other material, they can be used to create patterns and designs in art projects. The Cinnamon Girl collection was inspired by this childhood memory and the crafting movement of the 1970s.

materials:

(1) 4¼" wood piece for pendant (I repurposed an earring)

(3) 28mm wood triangle flatback cabochons

(24) 8mm x 6mm orange diamond plastic beads

(12) 12mm x 7mm violet teardrop plastic beads

(2) 15mm wood flat disc beads

(2) 11mm x 6mm wood triangle teardrop beads

(2) 10mm gold flower sequins

(3) 15mm gold oval sequins

(32) 5mm x 3mm turquoise donut or rondelle beads

(69) 5mm wood pink donut or rondelle beads

(5) 2.5mm SS9 Swarovski flatback rhinestones (Light Colorado Topaz)

16" memory wire necklace (.036 gauge)

(2) 1" gold-plated head pins

(2) 6mm gold-plated jump rings (.045 gauge)

(1) 10mm gold-plated jump ring (.064 gauge)

tools:

E6000 glue

Magic Wand

Memory wire shears

Round-nose pliers

Chain-nose pliers

Jump ring tool

process:

1. Using small pearl drops of glue, begin to pavé the focal pendant. (Pavé is a French word meaning stones are set extremely close together and cover an entire surface.) I like to start with the larger flat shapes and then build the pattern around them, keeping it symmetrical on both sides.

2. For smaller beads and crystals, use the Magic Wand to position everything perfectly. The amount of glue you use will depend on the shape and size of the beads. Don't worry if a little bit squeezes out or is visible; it will shrink and dry perfectly clear.

3. When attaching a sequin, add a micro pearl drop of glue on top of the sequin hole.

4. Place a crystal on top to hide holes and secure crystals.

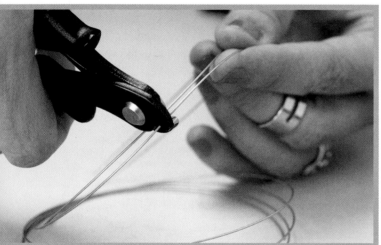

5. To make the memory wire choker, start by cutting the wire. I suggest using memory wire shears, as using regular wire cutters will damage them. These shears will also give you a perfect flush ending.

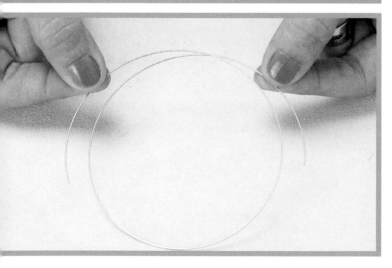

6. The length of the wire should be 16".

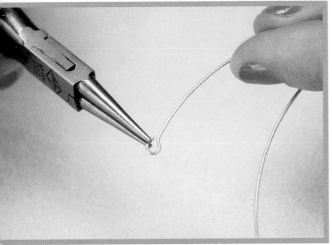

7. Make a small loop using the round-nose pliers. This part can be tricky, because memory wire is very strong and does not bend easily. Hold the wire as tightly as possible with a firm grip. Make a loop and then bend the "neck" of the loop back to create that pretty shape. Close the loop tightly but only until it "kisses," as you do not want to overlap the wire loop. These finishing touches are what give your pieces a polished and professional look.

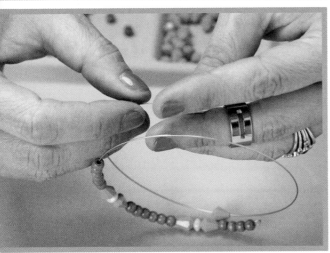

8. Using the same beads that you used to embellish the pendant, begin threading them onto the memory wire in a pattern that will complement the pendant. A good trick is to mark the center point of the wire with a marker so that you can begin mirroring your beadwork on the opposite side as soon as you reach this center mark. This is the spot where you will hang the pendant.

9. Once you reach the end of the wire, make another loop. I like to finish the ends of my memory wire with a little dangling charm on the loop. Make these charms by stacking two small beads on a head pin. Finish the head pin with a loop, and use the jump ring tool and chain-nose pliers to attach it to the wire with a small jump ring.

10. The final step is to attach the pendant in the center of the necklace using a heavy-gauge jump ring for added security.

Techno Tribal Pin Collar

For the Maasai women of Tanzania, making jewelry is a way of life. Their culture revolves around beading and the extreme body ornamentation that tell the stories of their families and traditions. Their delicately detailed and outrageously colorful beaded collars are made completely by hand with glass beads and found objects. This was the inspiration behind my Techno Tribal collection. My imaginary Maasai warrior women wear neon beads and carry laser-beam spears through a psychedelic landscape.

Inspirations

Taking a cue from the beautiful Maasai women, this project creates a collar out of beads and a found object that we all have in our sewing kit: safety pins! The safety pins give this collar its modern look by creating clean lines between the beads. They also give the collar structure when worn high on the neck.

materials:

(8) 2" long steel safety pins

36" Acculon wire (.018 diameter)

(8) 12mm acid yellow neon round Lucite beads

(9) 21mm acid pink neon round Lucite beads

(2) 4mm gold round beads

(2) 6mm gold round beads

(2) 8mm gold round beads

(12) 4mm silver round beads

(6) 6mm silver round beads

(4) 8mm silver round beads

(6) 10mm silver round beads

3" 8mm silver-plated link chain

8" 8mm silver-plated link chain

(2) sterling silver or sliver-finish crimp beads

(1) 6mm silver-plated jump ring (.045 gauge)

(1) 9mm silver-plated jump ring (.072 gauge)

(1) 9mm sterling silver or silver-finish lobster clasp

(1) 1" silver-plated head pin

tools:

Flat-nose pliers

Small cutter pliers

Alligator clips

Crimping pliers

Jump ring tool

Round-nose pliers

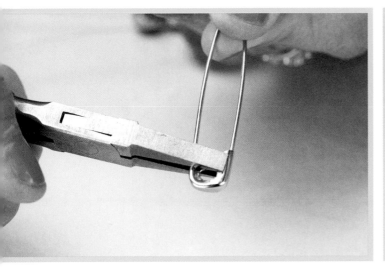
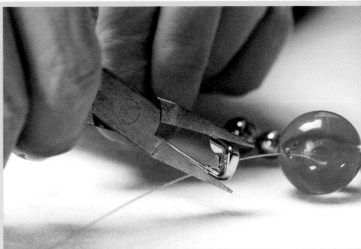

1. First, prepare the safety pins by pinching them in both directions with the flat-nose pliers. This will ensure that the bead wire does not slip through the jaw of the safety pin and that the pin can't open.

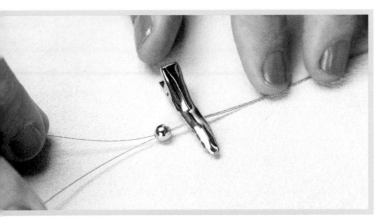

2. Cut two tandem pieces of the Acculon wire to the same size, approximately 18" each. Thread both wires through one small bead and secure them with an alligator clip. This will keep the wires from sliding through while you work.

3. Thread the beads onto the wire in a graduated pattern.

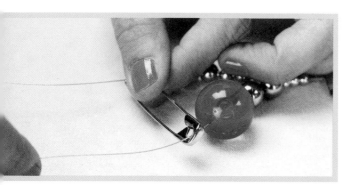

4. Thread the safety pin spacers onto the wires.

5. Repeat this pattern across to create the entire front piece of the necklace.

6. Now the front piece of the beadwork is complete.

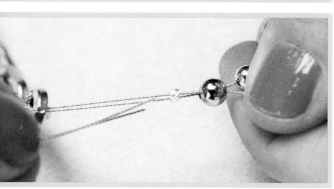

7. Pick either the 3" or 8" piece of chain to start. Having uneven pieces of chain on each end will allow the length of the necklace to be adjustable. Attach the front piece to the chain by first threading both wire strands through the crimp bead. Bring both strands around through the end chain link and back through the crimp bead and the first small bead. Pull the wires through, taking up the slack until the loop is the size of a small pearl.

8. Using the crimping pliers, clamp and fold the crimp bead.

9. Using small cutter pliers, cut the excess wire. Try to cut it as close to the inside of the bead hole as possible so the ends will tuck in. Be very careful when you do this so you don't cut the wrong strands and have to start over! Repeat this step by attaching the other piece of chain to the other side of the necklace.

10. Finish the shorter chain with a lobster clasp and jump ring by using the jump ring tool and pliers. Use the lobster clasp by clasping it directly to the chain. This will allow you to adjust the length of the necklace. Finish the longer chain with an accent bead by sliding the bead onto a head pin and making a loop at the top with round-nose pliers. Attach the accent bead to the end of the chain with a jump ring. This adds a nice detail to the back of the neck if it is visible.

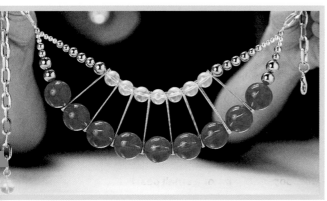

"Using safety
pins gives
jewelry a
modern
look with a
subversive twist."

Starlet
Sequin Choker

My Starlet collection celebrates the flamboyant style of the Roaring Twenties and the starlets that lit up the silver screen, nickelodeons, and arcades. Frolicking flappers or "Brinkley girls" would dance the night away, glittering head to toe in costume jewels. This was the moment when "it" girls everywhere liberated themselves with bobbed haircuts, short skirts, layers of glittering and gleaming necklaces, armfuls of jangling bracelets, ear fobs, and rings on every finger. Prudence Prim was the star of this era, brought to life by illustrator Nell Brinkley. Her wardrobe and costumes were the envy of every girl, and she often set the trends in fashion.

materials:

10" length x 1¾" wide white organza pull-cord ribbon

18½" delicate silver chain

(1) 25mm faux suede circular patch

(1) 1" embellished flower sequin trim

(1) 1" blue-foiled starburst sequin

(1) ¾" small flower sequin

(1) ⅝" sequin flower trim

(20) silver small star sequins

(1) 12mm sterling silver or silver-finish lobster clasp

(2) 6mm silver-plated jump rings (.051 gauge)

(1-2) silver oval sequins – *for the chain tag*

tools:

Needle and thread

Disposable baking pan or wax
  paper

Hot glue gun

Scissors

E6000 glue

Magic Wand

Chain-nose pliers

Jump ring tool

"I love using sequins because they give off a wonderful sparkling effect, like the shimmer on water."

process:

1. Start by making a ribbon rosette style corsage for the choker. Cut 18" to 20" of the pull cord ribbon. Gently pull the cord and gather the ribbon into a circular shape. I like using this ribbon because it's quick and easy, but you get the same effect with any ribbon by making a running stitch about ¼" from the edge.

2. Secure the ribbon by tying several knots and trimming the excess cord away.

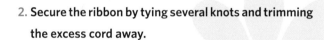

3. Stitch the two edges together to hold the circular shape.

4. Place the ribbon in a disposable baking dish or on wax paper, and lay the chain across the center. The chain should be slightly off center so one side is longer. This is because you want the corsage to be slightly off center when worn around the neck. It also allows the choker to be adjustable.

5. Apply a circle of hot glue, letting it fall onto the chain as well.

6. Quickly press the faux suede circular patch over the top to secure the chain.

7. Cut a piece of the flower sequin trim. This type of trim comes in all shapes and sizes and is used for apparel and costumes. Check the edges for any little imperfections and trim them away. This should be larger than the sequins we will layer on top to provide a focal frame.

8. Flip the ribbon over to the front and apply a ring of hot glue in the center.

9. Place the sequin trim in the center and press down.

10. Switch to E6000 glue now, as hot glue can melt sequins and is not advisable for the delicate gluing of smaller embellishments. To get the best results, use small pearl size-drops.

11. Continue to stack and glue the sequins.

12. Use the Magic Wand to pick up the stars and decorate the edges using mini pearl drops of glue to attach them.

13. Finish the shorter chain with a lobster clasp and jump ring by using the jump ring tool and chain-nose pliers. Finish the longer end by attaching a sequin or two to the jump ring.

CHAPTER 4

Bracelets

Sugar Skull Stretch Bracelet

One of my favorite holidays is Día de los Muertos, the Mexican Day of the Dead. My favorite place to get inspired for this special holiday is Olvera Street in downtown Los Angeles. In October and November, the tiled walkways of this vibrant street become a kaleidoscopic shrine to the afterlife and celebrations of loved ones departed and eternal love. Everywhere you look there are colorful Calaveras, sugar skulls, and marigolds, all symbolic of this delightful holiday.

Inspirations

I found these skulls at a local bead shop. They are made of a stonelike material called howlite and come in all the traditional brilliant "Día" colors. The fun part about this project is embellishing the little Calaveras skulls, giving them personality and making them your own.

materials:

(1) 30mm large skull bead

(2) 4128 10mm x 8mm Swarovski crystal stones (Fuchsia) – *for large skull eyes*

1½" length x ⅛" wide flat cording trim – *for large skull headband embellishment*

(11) 2028 SS9 Swarovski flatback crystals (Rose) – *5 for large skull headband embellishment and 6 for small skull eyes*

(2) mini embroidered rose embellishments

(2) 10mm plastic flowers

(10) 2028 Swarovski flatback crystals (SS16 Silver Shade, SS12 Topaz, and SS30 Light Rose AB) – *for medium skull eyes*

12" length 1mm jelly cord (such as Stretch Magic)

(5) 17mm medium skull beads

(3) 12mm small skull beads

(1) 28mm heart bead

(1) 16mm rose bead

(2) 5mm x 6mm blue donut or rondelle beads

tools:

E6000 glue

Magic Wand

Scissors

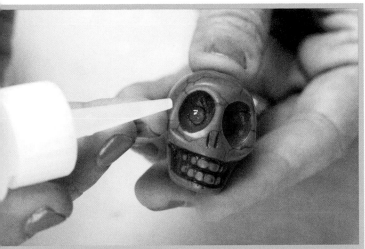

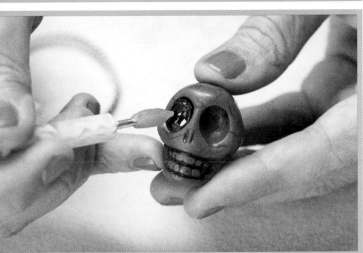

process:

1. **First, dress up the skull beads. Start by putting a small pearl drop of glue in the eye sockets of the large skull bead.**

2. **Using the Magic Wand, place the oval Swarovski crystals into the skull's eye sockets.**

3. **Now make the skull a headband by dotting glue along the flat cording trim.**

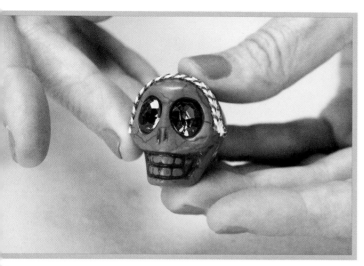

4. **Press it over the crown of the skull to create the band.**

5. Add the mini embroidered rose embellishments.

6. Dot the headband with five of the SS9 crystals.

7. Finish embellishing the smaller skull beads with the rest of the SS9 crystals and the plastic flowers.

8. Thread the beads onto the jelly cord in a random but deliberate pattern. Nothing is an accident; even a random pattern has to be thought out so that the beads create a story. Make sure you finish and knot the cord near the largest bead hole you can find so it can be tucked inside.

9. Knot the jelly cord no less than four times for security, trim the excess away, and pull the knot into the hole. Finish with a micro pearl drop of E6000 glue.

Barcelona Slide Cuff

When I was living in Barcelona years ago, I fell in love with the sculptural design and architecture of artist Antonio Gaudí. His kaleidoscopic use of color mixed with surrealism makes his work both bizarrely whimsical and strangely futuristic. In this project, the colorful swirls in the polymer clay and the crystals arranged in mosaic patterns are reminiscent of Gaudí's work.

Inspirations

This statement cuff is engineered like a vintage slide bracelet, but on a larger scale. The way the round beads roll between the slides make it uniquely comfortable for its size and scale.

materials:

Premo Sculpey oven-bake clay (5042 Black, 5040 Blue
    Translucent, 5392 Raw Sienna, and 5003 Denim)

(1) 40mm x 30mm oval crystal gemstone (Volcano)

(2) 25mm x 18mm rectangular crystal gemstones (Volcano)

(18) 8mm round howlite swirl beads

(14) 2028 SS30 Swarovski flatback crystals (Volcano)

(12) 2018 SS12 Swarovski flatback crystals (Sapphire AB)

(15) 12mm round howlite swirl beads

36" strand 1mm jelly cord cut into three 12" lengths
    (such as Stretch Magic)

tools:

Clay mat

Sculpey Super Slicer, razor
    blade, or X-Acto knife

Sculpey Etch 'N Pearl metal
    skewers

Magic Wand

Alligator clips

Small cutter pliers

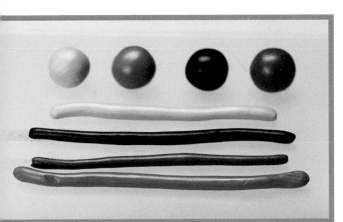

1. I want to make my Gaudí-inspired slides match the beautiful howlite swirled beads in this bracelet. To achieve this, we need to swirl these four clay colors together. First, break off one segment per color (the Premo clay bars have four segments). Now roll the clay into balls about the size of a silver dollar. Then roll each into a long snake shape.

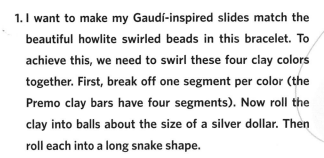

2. Twist the snakes together, then roll them into one snake. Roll this snake into a ball and repeat. You should twist and "taffy pull" the clay so the swirls get thinner each time. Now you have achieved the perfect swirl pattern.

3. Roll the clay into a log shape, making sure it is balanced on either side.

4. Using the rigid blade, slice the clay into three pieces, one larger and two smaller.

5. Now it's time to create the Gaudí-inspired bracelet slides. Roll each into a ball and shape. The shape of the slides should echo the shape of the stones you have chosen. Remember not to flatten the "slide" pieces too much. I like to leave them about ⅓" thick to allow for the larger crystals to be embedded. Gently press the crystals into the center of the slides and reshape the clay around them. This is the part that takes patience, but your pieces will look beautiful when they are done.

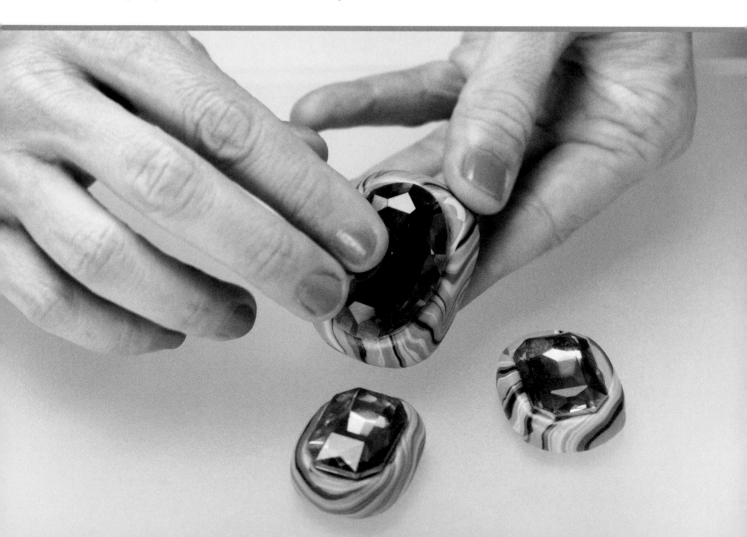

6. Using the Sculpey metal skewers, make three symmetrically positioned holes through to the other side. You may need to recheck the holes several times before baking to make sure they have not become blocked. Also make sure the holes are big enough to tuck the jelly cord knots into later.

7. Using the 8mm beads, gently dap the holes making a slight indentation. This creates a cup for the beads to sit in securely, and will help the jelly cord flow smoothly through the entire piece and support the weight of the slides.

8. Using the Magic Wand, use the flatback crystals to create a mosaic design around the larger stones. Make sure to press the stones into the clay far enough to create little seats for them to sit in securely.

9. Now the slides are ready for baking. Follow the instructions on the package. It is safe to bake them with the stones. Once they have cooled after baking, check to make sure all the stones are secure. I use an X-Acto knife and try to pop them out. If they come loose, I put a dab of glue in the seat and reset the stones to lock them into place.

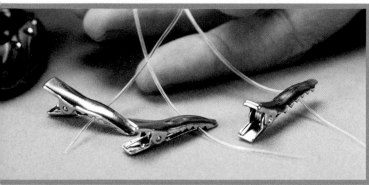

10. Cut three even strands of jelly cord about 10" long. Alligator clip the ends to keep the beads in place while you string the bracelet.

11. Assemble the bracelet by first stringing a small slider followed by two 8mm beads, the large slider, two 8mm beads, the other small slider, one 8mm bead, five 12mm beads, and one 8mm bead. Repeat this pattern on all three rows.

12. Knot the jelly cord four to six times, trim the ends, and tuck the knots into the slider holes.

"Using colorful gemstones in all shapes and sizes can create the impression of mosaic like the glass tiles on the beautiful Gaudi buildings in Barcelona."

Bow Tie Bangle

The bow tie has an androgynous fashion history being a staple in both women's and menswear. For women, bows are a symbol of femininity and sweetness. For men, they are a symbol of class and style. Charlie Chaplin wore a bow tie as a trademark of his gentleman tramp character. Singer Janelle Monae created a signature look with her modern take on the bow tie. With this project you can reinvent the bow tie once again—this time on your wrist! Wherever it appears, the bow tie always gives instant sophistication to any outfit.

Inspirations

We all have a forgotten bangle somewhere in that bottom drawer of our dresser at the back of our closet. Instead of sending it off to the thrift store, here is a quick and easy way to turn it into something new. Bows are a charming element I often use in my collections. The ribbon-wrapping method can be applied to everything from bangles to headbands and more.

materials:

(1) 3" Lucite bangle (any color)

60" length x ½" wide ribbon (Shimmering Nude)

4" wide black grosgrain ribbon bow

(28) 2028 SS5 Swarovski flatback crystals (Black Diamond)

(1) 3014 12mm Swarovski crystal button (Jet Hematite) – *for center of bow*

tools:

Hot glue gun

E6000 glue

Alligator clips

Magic Wand

"The bow tie is always in style and can be worn in endless ways."

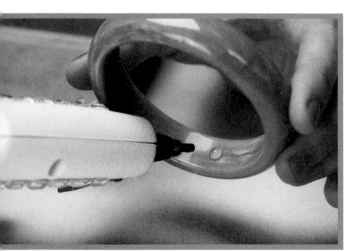

process:

1. Apply a medium-size pearl drop of hot glue on the inside of the bangle. Make sure it is nicely centered. Have the ribbon nearby, as you will need to move to step 2 quickly before the glue dries.

2. Press one end of the ribbon onto the glue drop firmly to make sure it adheres evenly to the bangle. For this bangle, which is about 1" wide, I am using approximately 60" of ribbon. Always give yourself extra ribbon if you are not sure. Running out of ribbon means starting over, and that's a waste of your precious design time.

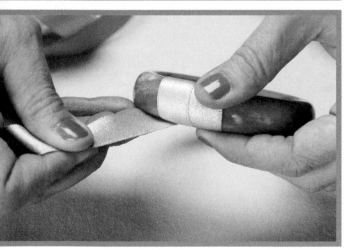

3. Begin wrapping the bangle with the ribbon at a slight angle. Be sure to keep the ribbon taut and smooth as you wrap it around. I like using ½" ribbon, which is just the right width for easy wrapping. If the ribbon is too thick, it will pucker.

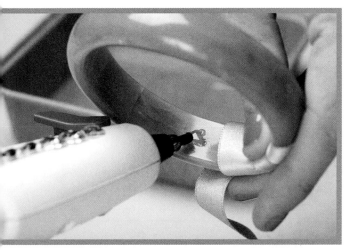

4. To lock the ribbon in place, apply small pearl drops of hot glue about 1" apart on the inside of the bangle as you wrap it.

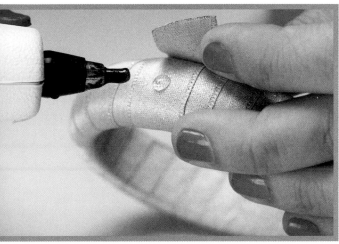

5. Secure the ribbon wrapping on the outside of the bangle with a small pearl drop of hot glue.

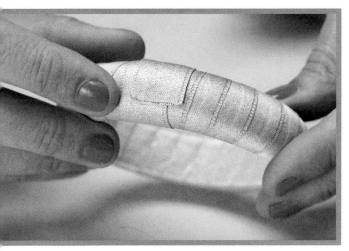

6. Don't worry about the seam of the ribbon showing, as you are going to hide it with the bow.

7. Place a mini pearl-size drop of the hot glue on the center of the ribbon seam and quickly press the center of the bow into place. Be careful to use only the correct amount of glue here, as you do not want the hot glue to show under the ribbon.

8. Switch to the E6000 glue. Place a mini pearl-size drop on the underside of the bow.

9. Use the alligator clips to hold the ribbon in place while it dries.

 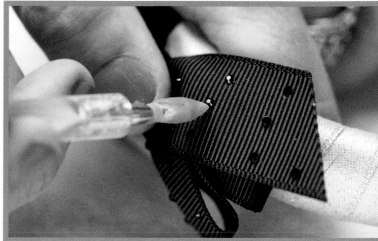

10. Give the bow a more opulent touch by dusting it with tiny crystals. First apply a micro-size drop of glue, and then use the Magic Wand to affix the 2028 SS5 crystals one at a time.

11. Place a small pearl-size drop of glue on the center of the ribbon.

12. Attach the crystal button.

CHAPTER 5

Earrings

Kashmir Gypsy Pom-Pom Earrings

Gypsy style is always a great source of inspiration for jewelry design. The entire culture of a tribe like the Lambani is based on the artful crafts they create and sell. Distinctive and exquisitely embroidered fabrics, costumes, and jewelry are all detailed with trademark coins, sequins, pom-poms, and colorful thread. Gypsy style is founded on a folkloric fantasy of painted caravans, crystal balls, and decadent dens of silk and gold that exists only in our imaginations.

Inspirations

Taking inspiration from this nomadic look, the earrings in this project feature materials that are unconventional in jewelry. You can have fun with this and try different materials or trims. If you don't have a twine-wrapped bead, you can easily make one with some hot glue and lightweight cording or yarn.

materials:

1 pair 6mm cupped earring posts

(2) 12mm round ivory Lucite beads

(2) 1" silver-plated head pins

(2) 6mm fire-polished chalk-white glass beads

(4) 2" silver-plated eye pins

(2) 22mm pink/gold textile wrapped wood beads

(4) 5500 9mm x 6mm faceted teardrop Swarovski crystals (Blue Zircon)

(4) 7mm round glass swirl beads

(2) 40mm pink pom-poms

(6) 18 or 20mm multicolored large hole paillette sequin discs (hole in sequin is 5mm)

(8) 4mm silver-plated jump rings (.032 gauge)

tools:

Permabond 2011 gel

Round-nose pliers

Flat-nose pliers

Jump ring tool

Chain-nose pliers

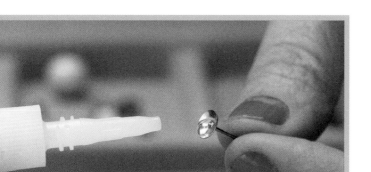

process:

1. Assemble the bead post for the top of the earring. Take the post with the dapped cup and place a small pearl drop of Permabond gel in the cup.

2. Quickly place the 12mm bead in the cup with the hole running vertically. Set aside to dry for about 1 minute.

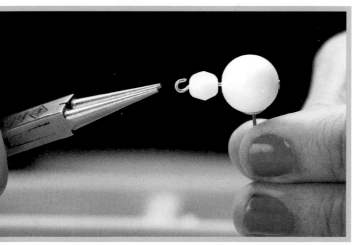

3. Thread a head pin through the 12mm bead along with one of the chalk-white glass beads and make a loop, leaving it open for later assemblage.

4. Thread the faceted teardrop crystals and the textile-wrapped wood bead onto an eye pin.

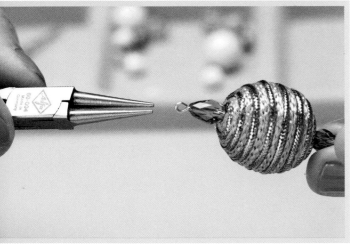

5. Use round-nose pliers to make a pretty loop on the end. You can leave it slightly open for later when you'll assemble all the parts.

6. Thread the glass beads and pom-pom onto another eye pin and leave the loop open as in step 3. Make sure you thread the eye pin through the center of the pom-pom where it is gathered so it cannot come loose.

7. Using the flat-nose pliers and jump ring tool, connect the paillettes together to create a flourish using jump rings. Loop each one to the next so that they fall in a cascading pattern. Leave the jump ring on the top paillette open for now.

8. With the chain-nose pliers, attach the section with the twine and teardrop beads to the bead post.

9. Continue attaching each section and finish with a paillette flourish.

"Use pom-poms to add charm and delight to your projects!"

Strange Delight Earrings

have always been obsessed with the striking elegance and whimsy of Bakelite jewelry. My Strange Delight collection recalls the comforting touch and luscious weight of this much-loved man-made material. In designing this collection, I drew inspiration from the world-renowned mobile artists Alexander Calder and Joan Miró. Here, the buttons are linked together in a ladder pattern and become floating discs, which give them a decidedly modern flair.

Inspirations

Through color and form, this project uses vintage buttons to simulate the look and feel of Bakelite. Buttons remind us of simpler times and sewing class. I collect buttons and store them in jars, as they always come in handy for a variety of projects.

materials:

(16) 5328 bicone 6mm Swarovski crystal beads (Black Diamond)

(10) 5328 bicone 6mm Swarovski crystal beads (Light Peach)

(10) 5040 rondelle 6mm Swarovski crystal beads (Erinite)

(16) 1" silver-plated eye pins

(2) 24mm yellow plastic buttons

(2) 25mm coral plastic buttons

(4) 15mm pearl white plastic buttons

1" length delicate silver-plated chain (½" for each earring)

1 pair titanium ear hooks

(2) 1" silver-plated head pins

(2) 12mm ivory round Lucite beads

tools:

Round-nose pliers

Small cutter pliers

Chain-nose pliers

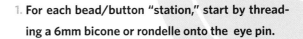

process:

1. For each bead/button "station," start by threading a 6mm bicone or rondelle onto the eye pin.

2. Thread through one buttonhole and then one additional bicone.

3. Using round-nose pliers, make a loop on the end of the eye pin, leaving it slightly open for assemblage later.

4. Repeat steps 1 to 3 using the other buttonhole, then repeat steps 1 to 4 to create three more stations for the earring.

5. Now you'll assemble the earring stations into a ladder. Simply hook each station together and close the eye pins with the chain-nose pliers.

6. Thread a bead onto the ear hook, use round-nose pliers to make a loop, and let it rest on top of the loop.

7. Cut three small links of the chain and attach the ear hook loop to the middle link. Attach the outer links to the eye pin loops at the top of the button ladder.

8. Thread the 12mm Lucite bead and a crystal bicone bead onto an eye pin and make a loop. Next, cut another three links of chain and attach the center link to the loop.

9. Attach the outer links to the bottom loops of the button ladder for the finishing touch.

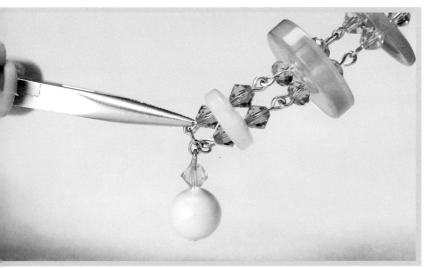

Sweet Shop Earrings

On a trip through Europe in the late 1990s, I found a defunct jewelry and ornament factory. After touring its dilapidated remains, I was led to a warehouse full of amazing treasures that had been passed up or forgotten long ago. Luckily for me, the warehouse contained hundreds of stacked boxes, each labeled delicately, and full of beautifully detailed resin flowers in an endless array of colors and styles. They were made with multiple molds and hand painted, a method that would be impossibly expensive to reproduce today. I purchased them all on the spot, had them sent back to Los Angeles, and use them in my collections to this day.

Inspirations

These confectionery flowers were the inspiration for the earrings in this project. The flowers I use here were found in a place just as unlikely: the 99-cent store! The simple use of crystals gives these earrings a distinctly retro look.

materials:

(2) 32mm blue plastic flowers (cut from plastic baby barrettes)

(2) 2028 SS30 Swarovski flatback crystals (Blue Zircon)

(10) 2028 SS16 Swarovski flatback crystals (Aquamarine)

(2) 8mm titanium flat pad earring posts and backs

tools:

Scissors

Small cutter pliers

220 grit sandpaper

E6000 glue

Magic Wand

"The vintage resin flowers found in that old factory inspired these pieces from our Floriculture collection."

process:

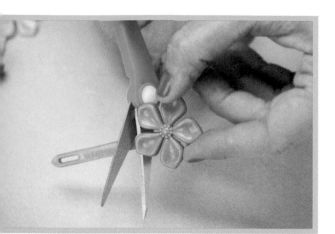

1. Use scissors to trim the barrette stems off the flowers.

2. Turn the first flower over and use the cutters to trim off any excess plastic parts.

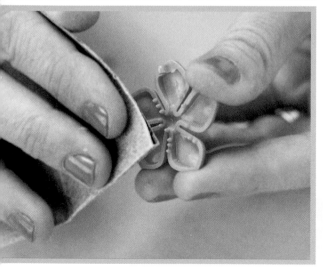

3. Use 220 grit sandpaper to smooth the back of the flower.

4. Place a small pearl of glue in the center of the flower.

5. Using the Magic Wand, place a SS30 crystal in the center of the flower.

6. At the edge of the petals, dot mini pearl-size drops of glue and affix the SS16 crystals.

7. Turn the flower over, add a medium-size pearl of glue, and attach the pad post. Let the glue dry thoroughly.

City Girl Hoop Earrings

I love big hoop earrings, and have done many different interpretations of this classic shape over the years. Hoops are playful and sophisticated; historically they are symbols of power and rank dating back to the Bronze Age. Pirates believed the magical powers of the metals in the hoops they wore would improve their eyesight and keep evil spirits away. In cinema, the bad or tough girl typically wears exaggerated hoop earrings. The hoops in this project are constructed with two sizes of memory wire, which makes them spin and sparkle, adding a surprise element to the design.

Inspirations

In the My Pretty collection campaign, our Dorothy starts out as an L.A. city girl, complete with big hoops, before she arrives in Oz. By simply threading Swarovski crystals onto memory wire, you get a beautiful circle of sparkles that can be created in endless patterns and designs. If you like your hoops on the smaller side, simply use a smaller loop of memory wire on the outside hoop.

materials:

10¼" large loop memory wire (.032 gauge)

6¼" small loop memory wire (.032 gauge)

(12) 3mm round silver-plated metal beads

(6) 4mm round silver-plated metal beads

(6) 5mm round silver-plated metal beads

(4) 6mm round silver-plated metal beads

(6) 8mm round silver-plated metal beads

(2) 10mm round silver-plated metal beads

(12) 5000 6mm round Swarovski crystals (Erinite)

(6) 5328 6mm bicone Swarovski crystals (Erinite)

(144) 5328 4mm bicone Swarovski crystals (Erinite)

(2) 2" silver-plated eye pins

1 pair titanium ear hooks

(2) 1" silver-plated head pins

tools:

Memory wire shears
Round-nose pliers

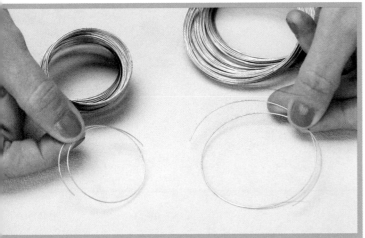

process:

1. Use the memory wire shears to cut about one and one-half circles of each size wire.

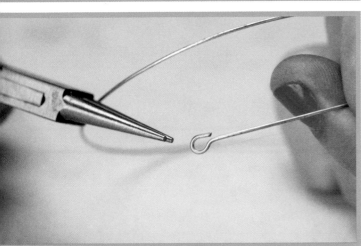

2. Use the round-nose pliers to make a horizontal loop on the end of the larger wire.

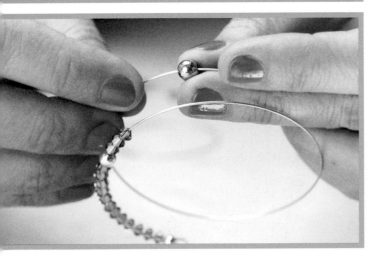

3. Thread the beads onto the larger hoop following the pattern pictured. Graduating the beads from small to large to small creates a perfect center of gravity.

4. Finish the hoop with another horizontal loop.

5. Repeat the same steps on the smaller hoop.

6. Thread the eye pin with the 6mm bicone and 3mm metal bead through the horizontal loops of the small hoop.

7. Continue threading the metal and bicone beads on the eye pin, and thread through the loops of the larger hoop.

8. Using the round-nose pliers, make a loop on the end of the eye pin and trim excess wire.

9. Thread a bead onto the ear hook and attach it to the eye pin.

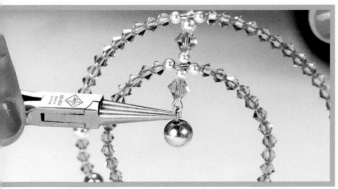

10. Thread an 8mm bead onto the head pin and make a loop. Attach it to the center loop.

"The hoop earrings from our L.A. City Girl collection were inspired by the style and culture of downtown Los Angeles."

• CHAPTER 6 •

Rings

Dollhouse Flowerpot Ring

When we were shooting the campaign book for the My Pretty/Wizard of Oz jewelry collection, I had two very willing volunteers to play the flowerpot girls in Munchkinland: my two daughters Chloe and Olivia. But there was more to the flowerpot story than the land of Oz. The flowerpot rings first appeared in my early collections back in the mid-1990s and were an instant hit. Everyone from Urban Outfitters to Macy's was ordering them by the hundreds and we could hardly keep up. Alfonso and I made every ring ourselves, and he spray-painted every candy-colored pot.

Inspirations

I am using felt flowers for this project, but you can also make them from fabric or polymer clay. The pots can be painted a single color, or you can use your imagination and embellish them in any number of ways.

materials:

For the ring:

(1) 2" pink felt flower (page 169)

(1) 1¼" green/pink felt flower (page 169)

8" length malleable craft wire (.036 gauge)

(16) 5mm x 3mm turquoise donut or rondelle beads

(1) 1" pink plastic button

(1) 14mm pink flatback plastic carved rose cabochon

(5) SS20 Swarovski crystals (Rose)

For the flowerpot:

1½" high x 1½" wide terracotta or wood mini flowerpot

(1) 6mm silver- or gold-plated jump ring (.045 gauge)

12" length string or cord (thin enough to fit through the hole in the bottom of the flowerpot)

Gloss enamel spray paint (protective goggles and face mask recommended)

Spray adhesive

(1) 25mm circle cut from sheet of grass green felt

½"-thick foam padding

(4) ½"-thick foam cubes cut from padding and used for flowerpot filler

tools:

Needle and thread

Scissors

Wire cutters

Hot glue gun

Round-nose pliers

Chain-nose pliers

E6000 glue

Magic Wand

Protective goggles and face mask

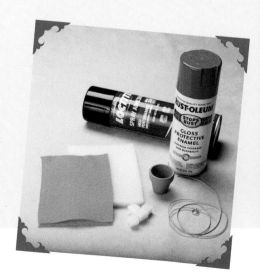

"Come out, come out wherever you are! Chloe and Olivia as the Flowerpot Girls from my Wizard of Oz collection book."

process for the large felt flower:

1. Making your own felt flower is easy. Two contrasting colors from the same color family make your flowers look more realistic and pretty. Cut out petals using the patterns supplied in this book (page 169), or draw and cut petal shapes in a ½" for the inner top petals and 1" for the bottom petals.

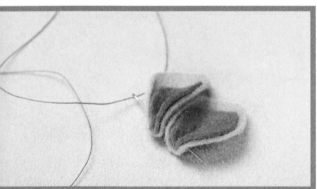

2. Layer the petals and secure them by folding at the base and stringing them together tightly with a needle and thread. Continue threading the petals until the flower is completed.

3. Knot tightly in the back, but make sure to leave the center of the flower unobstructed by thread or knots.

process for the small felt flower:

1. Cut out the inside green felt flower and tiny inner pink petals using the patterns supplied in this book (page 169).

2. With needle and thread, stitch the tiny inner pink petals to the green flower.

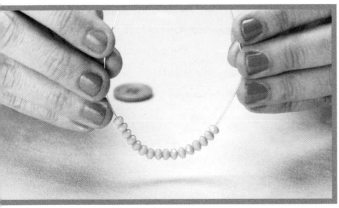

process for the ring:

1. Cut about 8" of craft wire and form it into a large "u" shape for the ring shank. Next, thread the rondelle beads onto the craft wire. If you are using the 5x3mm rondelles, you will need 16 beads to make an average size 7 ring. You can of course adjust the number of beads for a custom fit.

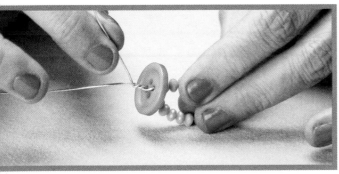

2. Thread the button with wire passing diagonally through two of the buttonholes.

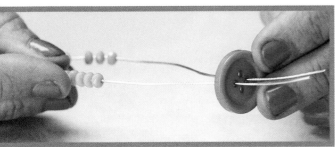

3. Take up any wire slack and shape the ring shank into a nice circle. Next, cross the wires and firmly twist them into a straight stem about 1" long.

4. Trim excess wire away from the stem.

5. The completed base of the flower ring should look something like this.

6. Pass the stem through the center of the large felt flower from the back. Add a medium to large pearl of hot glue depending on the size of the button and flower. Be careful not to use too much as it could ooze out. The beauty of using a button for the base here is that it acts as a cup to hold the flower and conceal the glue.

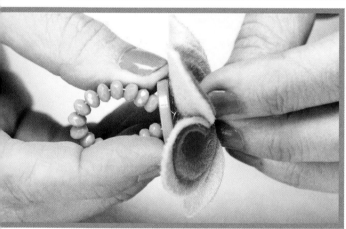

7. Press the flower firmly into the hot glue and hold it for about 10 to 15 seconds until secure.

8. Using round-nose pliers, create a loop in the stem and bend it back toward the flower.

9. Fold the loop down flush against the flower center using chain-nose pliers.

10. Place a small pearl drop of hot glue over the stem loop.

11. Press the small felt flower into place. Now switch to E6000 glue and attach the plastic carved rose cabochon.

12. Using the E6000 glue and the Magic Wand, add the flatback crystals to the petals with a micro pearl drop of glue.

process for the flowerpot ring holder:

1. Thread the cord and jump ring through the flowerpot. The jump ring will be on the inside of the flower pot. Hang the flowerpot from a clothesline outdoors or in a well-ventilated area. Hold the paint can about 6" away from the pot and then give the pot a good spin as you paint it. Be sure to move the can slowly up and down to coat the entire pot and some of the inside too. (This is a trick that Alfonso developed when we got a huge order from Macy's N.Y. for their Easter windows one year. We had to make a thousand of these pots in a few days.) Always wear a face mask and protective goggles when using spray paint even if you don't do it very often. If you use spray paint often, you should invest in a good paint respirator.

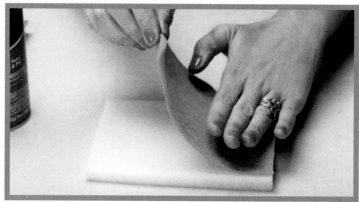

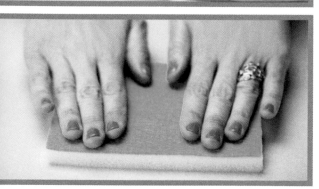

2. Now you'll make the insert/ring holder. Using spray adhesive, follow the instructions on the bottle to fuse the felt and foam together. Press firmly and smooth out the wrinkles. Let it dry for about 30 minutes.

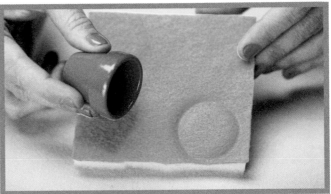

3. To create the shape for the ring insert, take the mini pot and press it on the felt surface to make an impression. Doing this avoids pen marks on the felt from tracing around the pot and is more accurate.

4. Cut out the circle, being careful not to cut it too small. Don't worry if it is not a perfect circle, as we will be tucking the edges in later.

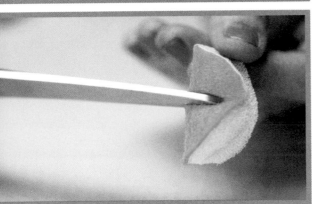

5. Fold the circle in half and with the tip of the scissors make a ½" slit.

6. Now assemble the flowerpot by pressing three or four of the foam cubes inside at the bottom of the pot. Line the inside of the pot about ¼" down with E6000 glue.

7. Take the ring insert and bunch it together, then release it inside the pot. Using the Magic Wand, tuck in the edges of the felt carefully. Allow it to dry for an hour before placing the ring into the pot.

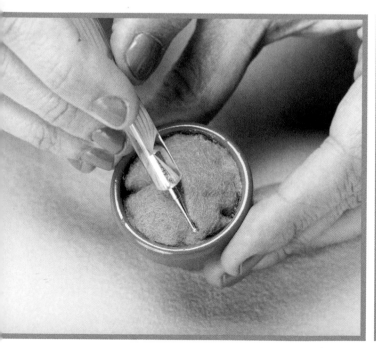

patterns:

"Felt gives color a unique depth and dimension. Here we created giant felt flowers as the backdrop for our Wizard of Oz Munchkinland."

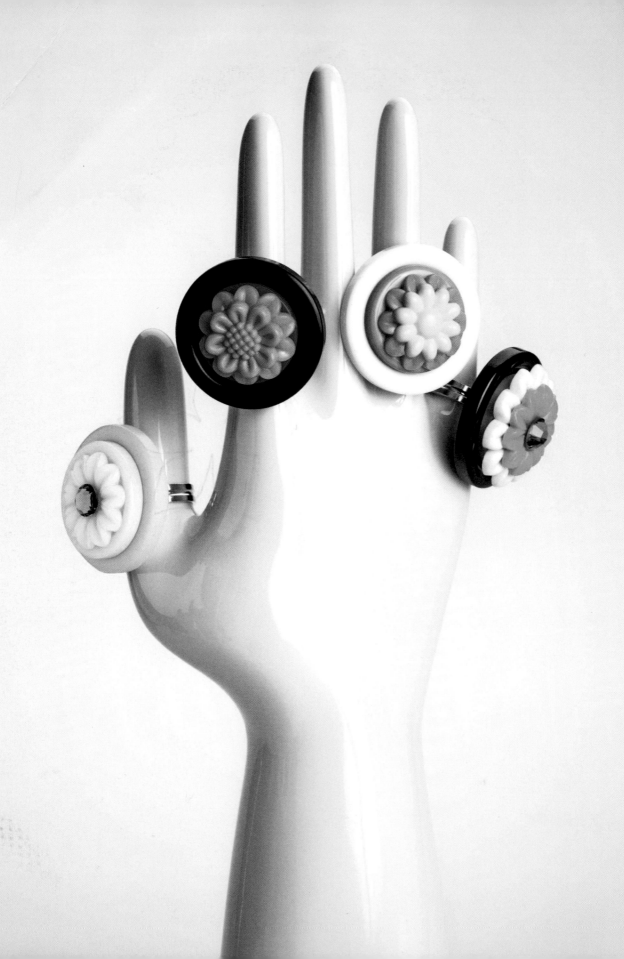

Fantastic Plastic Mod Ring

love everything Lucite, resin, and preciously plastic. The first plastics were developed for billiard balls (to imitate ivory) and celluloid movie film. But soon this incredibly versatile material found its way into the fashion world, and suddenly everything from jewelry to buttons to sunglasses took on a modern, colorful look that was not possible with traditional materials. In the 1960s, plastic rings were everywhere and were seen as the perfect graphic finishing touch to any Mod look.

Inspirations

Stacked plastic buttons and flowers from plastic baby barrettes make this project quick and easy. If you don't have a metal ring shank, check out the beaded one we made for the Dollhouse Flowerpot Ring (page 163); you can use that technique to make a similar shank here.

materials:

- (1) 38mm black plastic button
- (1) 25mm pink plastic button
- (1) 19mm plastic flower (cut from plastic baby barrette)
- (1) 25mm plastic flower (cut from plastic baby barrette)
- (1) Adjustable metal shank ring with 20mm gluing pad

tools:

Scissors

Small cutter pliers

E6000 glue

"The Mod statement ring is meant to be worn alone, so the bigger the ring the better!"

process:

1. Use scissors to trim the barrette stems off the flowers.

2. Turn the flower over, and use the small cutter pliers to trim off any excess plastic parts.

3. You are going to stack the buttons and plastic flowers wedding cake-style to create the ring. Start with the largest button by dotting with small pearl-size drops of glue.

4. Affix the next smaller size button into place.

5. Use another medium-size drop of glue.

6. Now stack the plastic flowers, adding glue in between.

7. Allow this to dry for at least half an hour.

8. After applying a large pearl-size drop of E6000, affix the ring shank into place and allow it to dry overnight before wearing.

"I chose a black
button for the base
of this ring as it
makes the flowers
pop in a psychedelic
and colorful way."

Paris Apartment Cocktail Ring

One of the first pieces of jewelry I ever made as a child was a gumball-shaped ring out of polymer clay. Many years later I would find myself living in Paris during my modeling career and rediscovering this amazing material. At night in my tiny apartment above the Rue Mouffetard Market, I would handcraft chunky beaded necklaces, chandelier earrings, and colossal-sized crystal cocktail rings. On weekends, I would comb the isles of the Clignancourt flea market looking for old jewelry with big stones that I could repurpose for my rings. On shoots, stylists, photographers, and other models would buy them right off of me. The over-sized cocktail ring is one of my favorite accessories because they can instantly dress up any outfit, and they never go out of style.

Inspirations

Taking a simple ball of clay and turning it into a couture fashion cocktail ring in minutes is instant fashion gratification at its best! The secret of this project is the swirling of the clay colors to create beautiful patterns and designs. No two rings are ever the same!

materials:

Premo Sculpey oven-bake clay

  (5513 Purple, 5519 Bronze, 5504 Fuchsia, and 5033

  Orange)

(1) 1" square faceted crystal gemstone

tools:

Clay mat

Clay detailing tool

Sharpie

Ring sizer (optional)

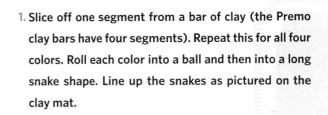

process:

1. Slice off one segment from a bar of clay (the Premo clay bars have four segments). Repeat this for all four colors. Roll each color into a ball and then into a long snake shape. Line up the snakes as pictured on the clay mat.

2. Now take all four snakes and roll them into a candy stick.

3. Twist the clay candy stick, roll it into a ball, and then roll it into a snake again.

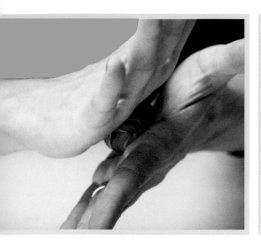  

4. Once more roll the clay into a ball, then roll it into a snake. "Taffy twist" and pull the snake and roll it into a final ball. You will now see how all of that twisting and rolling has made a beautiful marbleized pattern in the clay.

5. Begin shaping the ball into a ring by pinching one-half of the clay to form the shank, while squaring off the front to form the crown where the crystal will go.

6. Place the stone into the crown. Press the stone into the ring by placing it face down on the clay mat and applying a steady pressure while gently shaping the crown around the stone.

7. Now make the shank (the part that fits around your finger). Start by using a clay detailing tool to pierce the clay from both sides. Use a circular motion to increase the circumference of the shank opening.

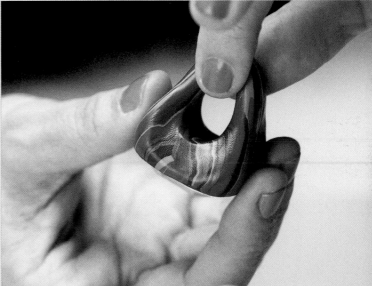

8. Now take a Sharpie and, using the bottom end, continue to make the shank opening bigger. Gently pull the lower part of the shank and continue to shape it. Be careful here not to make the shank too large; once that happens you have to start over. Also be careful not to make the walls of the ring shank too thin, as this could cause the ring to break after baking. A good rule is to leave the ring wall about 5-8mm thick.

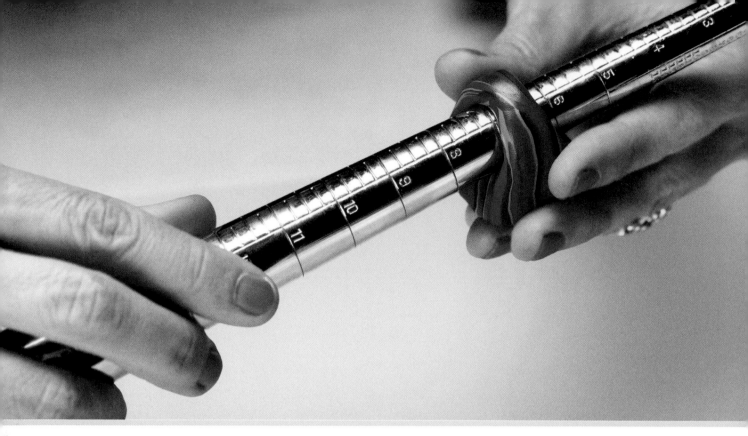

9. If you have a ring sizer, this is the best way to make sure your ring is the size you want it to be before you bake it.

10. Put the ring in the oven and bake as directed on the clay packaging.

"Big and colorful rings are very chic, like wearable art. I like the way they look on the hand, sparkle in the light, and the conversations they start."

Jubilee Stretch Ring

Gobstoppers; sputniks; and jewelry from the 1940s and '50s. Beaded cluster jewelry came into fashion thanks to Miriam Haskell, who masterfully designed beaded jewelry like nobody before. With a love for the organic and the whimsical, Haskell and her partner Frank Hess built a jewelry empire and began laying the foundation for costume jewelry's collectability. These splendid rings seemed plucked right off the hand of Auntie Mame and capture the spirit of costume jewelry from this time.

Inspirations

Jubilee stretch rings are one of my favorite things to make. They are quick, easy, and fun. When you tie them up, the beads form a bundle "blossom" that becomes the crown of the ring. Different-shaped beads give different-shaped blossoms! Make them in every color for every outfit or one for each day of the week.

materials:

(10) 1" silver-plated head pins

1" length 1mm jelly cord (such as Stretch Magic)

(5) 10mm round faceted glass beads (miscellaneous colors)

(2) 12mm round faceted glass beads (miscellaneous colors)

(1) 12mm violet onion-shaped bead

(1) 12mm acid pink neon round Lucite bead

(1) 3400 8mm square Swarovski crystal bead (Crystal AB)

(About 18) 5mm x 3mm donut or rondelle glass beads
   (miscellaneous colors)

tools:

Round-nose pliers

Small cutter pliers or scissors

E6000 glue (optional)

process:

1. First prepare the bead charms by threading each bead onto an eye pin and using round-nose pliers to make a loop.

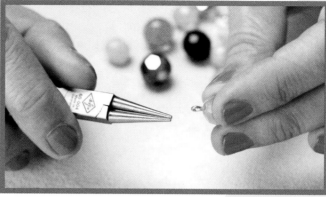

2. Thread about 10 bead charms onto the jelly cord.

3. Tie the beads into a cluster by knotting the jelly cord about four times.

4. String the smaller rondelle beads onto the remaining cord. Use about 18 beads for a standard size 7 ring.

5. Finish by tying four knots as close to the middle of the bead cluster as possible.

6. This can get a little tricky as the smaller beads will want to join the party and creep into the knotting zone, so use your thumb to hold them back while you tie the knots.

7. Trim the remaining cord, but not too close to the knot or else it may unravel.

CHAPTER 7

Hair
Accessories

Petit Chapeau

These petit chapeaus (or "little hats") are such a highly concentrated dose of fun that as soon as you walk through the door, everyone knows the party has begun. They originally gained popularity in the nineteenth century by adding a whimsical allure to Victorian dress. Sometimes called fascinators or cocktail hats, they are purely decorative and function more as a headband or hair ornament than a hat. The petit chapeau for this project takes inspiration from vintage circuses, penny arcades, and sunbleached carnivals.

Inspirations

Festooned with worn ribbons and a circus-themed "cockade," this party hat is a precious treasure to create and add to your collection. You might love it so much you will want to make one for every special occasion and holiday.

materials:

(1) Mini costume top hat with elastic band

DecoArt Acrylic paint in Indian Turquoise and Baby Blue

DecoArt crackle finish

10" length x 2" wide pink grosgrain ribbon

(1) 1" embroidered star patch

(1) 40mm long x 38mm wide silver-finish oval metal bezel frame

3" length square aquamarine Swarovski crystal chain

Blue feather trim

12" length x ½" wide pink velvet ribbon

(1) ¼" elephant bead Lucite charm (or selected charm)

(1) 5mm silver-plated jump ring (.032 gauge)

12" length x 1" wide ivory with pink detail canvas ribbon

tools:

Disposable paintbrush

Fine-grit sanding block or sandpaper

Needle and thread

Scissors

E6000 glue

Small cutter pliers

Hot glue gun

Chain-nose pliers

Jump ring tool

"Tiny Swarovski crystals dusted across the fishnet veil on this Victorian Punk fascinator give it a dramatic and unexpected flair."

1. Paint the mini top hat with the Indian Turquoise color. Let dry. Then switch to the Baby Blue color and paint another coat. Allow each color to dry thoroughly in between each coat. Next apply the crackle paint to give the mini top hat a distressed texture. Once it is completely dry (I like to give it a full day), take the fine-grit sandpaper block and very, very lightly rub it across the crown and brim to lightly distress the edges.

2. Usually these costume hats have a flat brim, so I like to give mine a more authentic look by gently curving up the sides and using the chin strap to hold it in place over-night.

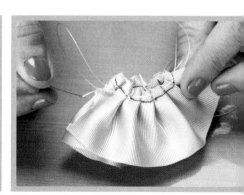

3. Next you'll need to make the cockade ribbon rosette decoration. To ruffle the ribbon, make a running stitch (using a double strand of thread) about ¼" from the edge. Gently pull the thread and gather the ribbon into a circular shape. Fold the ends into the center and stitch the open ends together. Make some small stitches to keep the rosette folded permanently in half.

4. I made these embroidered patches with my Babylok embroidery machine here at the factory, but you can get a similar look by hand stitching a patch or sourcing something similar.

5. Glue the cameo patch into the metal bezel frame with the E6000.

6. Draw a line of glue around the edge of the cameo and trim it with the crystal chain. Make sure to push the crystals together as you glue them down so that they frame the cameo nicely. Trim the excess chain away using the small cutter pliers.

7. Sew the frame securely onto the half rosette.

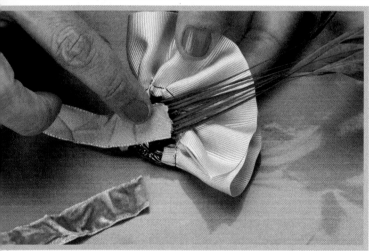

8. Turn the rosette over and hot glue about 1" of the feather tape to the back followed by the velvet ribbon.

9. Using the chain-nose pliers and jump ring tool, attach the elephant bead or selected charm to the frame with the jump ring.

10. Using a pearl-size drop of hot glue, lay down the ivory with pink detail canvas ribbon first and wrap it around the entire hat top, affixing it snugly with more hot glue.

11. Attach the cockade with a large pearl-size dollop of hot glue. Run the pink velvet ribbon around the side over the larger ribbon and attach it behind the cockade with more hot glue.

"The best accessories
are those meant
purely to delight."

Broken Treasure Hair Jewels

Before I went pink I went short. Taking a turn with a Jean Seberg "do'" was fun, but growing it out was not. I needed something pretty to pin it back, but there was nothing but bland and boring bobbies in the marketplace. To get my tresses the sparkle fix they needed I had to make my own glittering gems, and thus my first collection of hair jewelry was born. Back then I wore them with my velvet babydoll dresses and Dr. Martens (can't you just hear Blind Melon playing in the background?), and they were an instant hit. The first hair jewels I made were just like these, using any sparkly bits that I had around.

Inspirations

Now is the time to get out that box of tangled trinkets and make something amazing from those broken bits.

materials:

(1) 1" or 1½" silver French barrette

2" length x ¼" wide black sheer grosgrain ribbon

About 1" length 6mm square Swarovski crystal chain
   (Black Diamond)

About 1" length 8mm round Swarovski crystal chain (Rose)

(1) Swarovski crystal flower (or any costume jewelry flower)

tools:

E6000 glue

Scissors

Alligator clips

Heavy-duty cutter pliers

Small cutter pliers

Fine sandpaper

"Hair jewelry can also be clipped on a ribbon to create the look of a headband."

process:

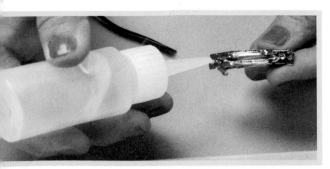

1. Cover the surface of the barrette with glue.

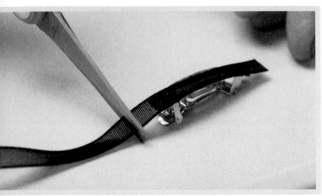

2. Lay the ribbon across the top, allowing about ½" to hang over either side.

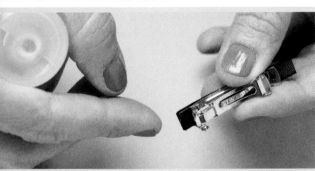

3. With a small pearl-size drop of glue, fold the ribbon over the edges and secure it with alligator clips. Let dry.

4. Trim any excess metal parts off the broken jewelry pieces.

5. **Clip two segments of the Swarovski crystal chain in each size.**

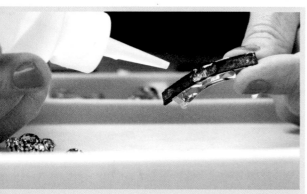

6. Using the sandpaper, lightly distress the backs of the jewelry pieces and crystal chain for better adhesion.

7. Place a small to medium pearl-size drop of glue on the center of the barrette and affix the broken jewelry piece.

8. To finish, glue the crystal chain pieces on either side of the centerpiece with small pearl-size drops of glue.

Mucha Muse Headband

In Paris at the turn of the century, the Art Nouveau movement enveloped the city in organic shapes and floral motifs. The artist at the center of this movement was Alphonse Mucha, whose magical muses seemed to float from the canvas dressed like goddesses in flowing dresses and ornamental "fillet" style headpieces. Art Nouveau is possibly my favorite design inspiration; elements of this style can be found in my collections season after season.

Inspirations

This project is completely hand sewn, using millinery flowers that can be sourced online or at flea markets. To get the exact shape you want for the larger focal flower on this piece, you can cut the flowers apart into sections and stack them together.

materials:

(1) 4½" silk velvet green millinery flower

(1) 3" silk velvet plum brown millinery flower

(2) 1½" silk velvet plum millinery flowers

(3) 5000 8mm round Swarovski crystal beads (Black Diamond,
Amethyst, and Aquamarine)

(2) 1" gold-plated head pins

(2) 5500 9mm x 6mm faceted teardrop Swarovski crystal drop beads
(Amethyst)

(5) 5mm gun-metal jump rings (.020 gauge)

(3) 6401 12mm octagon Swarovski crystal drop beads (Topaz)

2½" length 3mm gun-metal chain

(1) 1¾" gun-metal ornate loop pendant – *to construct the decoratif*

19" elastic velvet plum ribbon

(1) 1½" silk velvet green millinery flower

(7) small gold star sequins

(7) 5000 3mm round Swarovski crystal beads (Aquamarine)

tools:

Needle and thread

Scissors

Round-nose pliers

Jump ring tool

"Just like the girls in Mucha paintings, our model Lydia Hearst glows in layers of opulent hair ornaments and jewelry."

1. I couldn't find the exact size plum brown flower that I needed for this project, so I simply snipped the flower apart and will use the part that I need.

2. To create the base for the focal flower on the headband, layer the green millinery flower, the plum brown millinery flower, and one of the plum millinery flowers.

3. With the needle and thread, sew the stacked flowers together.

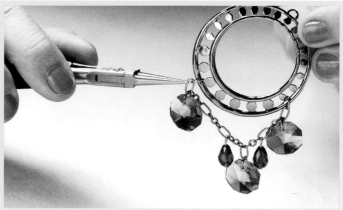

4. Thread the 8mm bead into the center of the flowers and tie off securely in the back.

5. Make the bead charms by threading an amethyst bead onto a head pin. Finish the head pin with a loop. Attach a jump ring to the topaz octagon drop beads using round-nose pliers. Attach the bead charms to the chain using the photo as a guide. Finally, attach the chain to the two points on the loop pendant using the jump rings.

6. Slide the loop pendant around the center flower and sew it tightly into place.

7. Measure your head and cut the velvet ribbon accordingly. Since it is a stretch ribbon, cut it slightly smaller than your head measurement. Cross stitch the two ends together securely. Try on the band and make sure it fits comfortably before you proceed.

8. Sew the flower to the headband securely.

9. Add the additional flowers to the front of the head-band, sewing one of the 8mm beads into the center. Before you sew on the flowers, determine where they will be positioned when the band is stretched.

10. Sew the sequin stars on using the 3mm crystal beads to secure them. Position the stars evenly between the flowers across the crown of the headband.

"Try using flowers
made of fabric,
linen, lace, or
leather. Layering
different materials
creates dimension
and interest."

CHAPTER 8

Other Accessories

Acid Cameo Western Belt Buckle

Neon showdown at the laser beam corral! Anyone who knows me well knows that I have a cowgirl heart having seen my share of fairgrounds during my horseshow days. I love western belts and have collected many over the years. This has led to the many whimsical and fairy-tale style buckles I have designed for my collections. Western buckles can incorporate any theme you want, and making your own creates the ultimate statement accessory.

Inspirations

Inspired by my classic Acid Cameo collections, this project juxtaposes unusual themes—Rococo and the old West—and gives the basic buckle a psychedelic makeover using polymer clay. The beauty of using this material is that it allows us to mimic the look of tooled leather.

materials:

Premo Sculpey oven-bake clay (5022 Wasabi, 5523 Candy Pink, and 5040 Blue Translucent)

1½" silver western style blank oval rope edge buckle

Sculpey Super Elasticlay Moldmaker (2½ times bigger than the size of the object you wish to mold)

Cornstarch or olive oil for mold release (optional)

(2) 3700 12mm flower-shaped Swarovski crystal beads (Topaz A/B)

tools:

Acrylic clay roller

Clay mat

Sculpey texture maker—*for the lace pattern*

Clay detailing tool

Clay molds

E6000 glue (optional)

Sculpey Glaze (optional)

{ "Belt buckles are not just for jeans. I love wearing them with vintage dresses or pencil skirts." }

process:

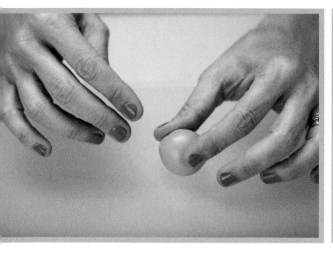

1. Work about one and one-half bars of the blue polymer clay into a ball. Then roll it out with the clay roller into an oval shape.

2. Place the shaped clay onto the surface of the buckle.

3. Place the texture maker on top of the clay and press down firmly so the design is deep and defined. Lift the sides periodically to make sure the clay has blanketed the entire surface of the buckle face.

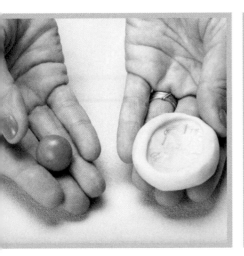

4. To make a cameo and frame using polymer push molds, see pages 53-54.

5. Place the cameo and frame in the center of the buckle face and gently press so they adhere to the surface of the textured clay. Be careful not to press too hard or you will lose details on the molded pieces.

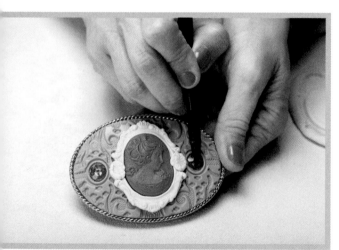

6. Now add some sparkle by pressing the crystal beads into the textured clay. What I love about this lace pattern is that it naturally creates a frame for the crystal beads.

7. Put the entire buckle in the oven and bake as directed on the clay packaging. After the buckle has baked and is completely cooled, you may need to pop the entire clay portion out of the buckle face and glue it back in with E6000, as the clay sometimes does not provide enough adhesion to the metal. If you prefer a glossy finish, just brush a coat of Sculpey Glaze evenly over the baked and cooled clay. This will also protect the surface of the buckle.

Sparkle Factory Spectacles

It's time to make a spectacle of yourself! The first sparkled specs appeared on the fashion scene in the 1950s when surrealist fashion designer Elsa Schiaparelli introduced a collection of sunglasses decorated with floral resin motifs and glittering jewels. Recently, embellished eyewear has come back into fashion and has been seen on the catwalks in Paris, Milan, and London. I started making these fantastical frames for fun around the factory and to wear for eye protection when cutting metal parts. Soon everyone wanted a pair! This is the perfect project to make with friends. Everyone brings an old pair of glasses for a "social spectacle" party—the photo ops after are the best part!

Inspirations

Highly collectible frames are hard to come by these days, but look them up online for some real eye candy inspiration. The secret to these spectacles is in the way you space the cabochons. If they're too far apart, they could become loose and fall off. For additional support, glue the cabochons and jewels next to each other like a puzzle. If you don't have any flower cabs on hand, try making some with polymer clay.

materials:

1 pair plastic clear eyeglasses or sunnies

(2) 18mm flower-shaped Lucite or resin cabochons

(7-10) 8-10mm flower-shaped Lucite or resin cabochons

31" length 4mm powder-coated metal chain (optional)

(2) 6mm silver-plated jump rings (.045 gauge) (optional)

tools:

Protective goggles and face mask
(if using drill)

Drill press, electric drill, or
Dremel rotary tool (optional)

Styrofoam disc, paper, or cups
(optional)

Hot glue gun

Chain-nose pliers (optional)

Jump ring tool (optional)

process:

1. Using a drill or Dremel, make holes in each temple toward the front of the spectacles to hang the chain later. Be sure to wear protective goggles and a face mask when drilling. If you don't own a drill or Dremel, you don't have to add the chain.

2. I like to use a Styrofoam disc for projects like this to hold glasses in place while I bejewel them.

3. Add a small pearl drop of hot glue in the corner and quickly place the largest flower.

4. Line a bit of hot glue along the top of the frame (be very careful not to get the glue on the lenses), and add another smaller flower.

5. Continue across the bridge and repeat on the opposite side. Remember that hot glue dries quickly, so you need to plan out the design before you start. I would also recommend using E6000 glue if you are making a really special pair, or using crystals in the design.

6. If attaching the chain to the frame, connect the jump rings to the chain and the temples by using chain-nose pliers and a jump ring tool.

· CHAPTER 9 ·

Wearing Jewelry

Play Dress-up Every Day

L et's think outside the jewelry box and discover the fashion superpowers of jewelry and accessories. Giving sparkle to your style means more than just jewelry. Think of that "sparkle" as touches in your wardrobe that create your signature look. When we get dressed every day we become our own billboard, showing the world who we are by what we wear. Create your own signature style and make a statement!

This does not mean being over the top and dressing like a cupcake. I am not suggesting that you show up at the office tomorrow wearing your new Petit Chapeau (well, maybe I am!); it just means taking the time to dress for the world and express your personal style. Obviously I am an advocate for looking different, and jewelry is the easiest and most effective way to make a style statement. It is also a great way to stretch your wardrobe and change things up. You can wear one outfit many different ways and dress it up or down with your accessories.

The way you adorn yourself every day, whether you pile bracelets from your wrist to your elbow or wear just a single ring, defines your style. I would describe my jewelry style as generally noncommittal; I want to be free to try something new and always keep evolving. But sometimes I find myself in a more monogamous relationship with a particular stack of bracelets, or that one great cocktail ring that works with everything. This is when I need to remind myself to break out! The secret is knowing how to wear your jewelry and experimenting with what works for you.

Accessorizing Rules

Minimalist, maximalist, and everything in between! Here are a few of my personal accessorizing suggestions:

JEWELRY IS THE MAIN EVENT, NOT THE SIDESHOW!

Choose an outfit that works with your jewelry. Sound backwards? That's because fashion dictators have told us forever that accessories are, well, just that, accessories. Well, I guess I never got the memo! Let's forget those silly rules and put our accessories in the driver's seat. You might be thinking of wearing your Paris Apartment Cocktail Ring tonight (how exciting is that!?), so choose the perfect dress to complement it. This is an exercise in thinking differently about how we dress, and to me is much more fun. For this red-carpet event I wanted to wear a big stack of bracelets on each arm, so I chose this Ann Demeulemeester minimal sheath dress to offset the drama created by the bracelets.

"Let your jewelry style become your personal trademark."

ACCESSORIZE HARMONIOUSLY:

I am a maximalist by nature. I like to pile it on, clutter it up, and push the envelope right to the edge, but I always make sure my pieces work together. If your earrings are fighting with your Cinnamon Girl Bib Necklace for attention, you have to choose sides.

Accessorizing harmoniously means creating balance. For example, if you are wearing big earrings, skip the necklace and offset your jewelry look by wearing a statement cocktail ring. On the flipside, don't be afraid of wearing too much. Sometimes too much is just the right amount; the biggest fashion crime is to be boring.

MAKE A STATEMENT:

In a minimal mood? Then let one great piece of jewelry do all the talking. Think of Coco Chanel's pearls, Madeleine Albright's metaphoric pins, Courtney Love's tiaras, or Liberace's rings; let the pieces you choose convey your mood. Choosing an accessory look that works for you and wearing it devotedly in different colors and styles can become your personal trademark.

GET CREATIVE WITH USE OF COLOR:

Making an accessory statement with a single color family like bright turquoise earrings and bracelets to contrast with your fuchsia dress is the kind of fashion dare we like to take head on. Try layering your jewelry in graduating shades of the same color, or color-blocking in complementary colors like pink with orange, or black with white. Maybe you have a signature color? Make it iconic by wearing a bit of that color every day. A red bangle today, red chandelier earrings tomorrow, red nail polish this weekend, and a red hat next week.

CLUSTER AND COLLAGE:

You know all of those beautiful vintage brooches, tie tacks, and stickpins you have been collecting? Wearing one can be fun, but wearing a bunch at once can create an interesting focal point to your outfit. I have some great pins from the '60s that my mom gave me, and I will sometimes put them on a cloche or down the entire lapel of a vintage jacket.

DON'T FOLLOW TRENDS, SET THEM:

This is the part where you get really creative and come up with new ways to wear your jewelry. Try one big earring with a small stud in the other or mismatched earrings. How about wearing a tiara with your jeans and T-shirt to the grocery store? Why not? Life should be about playing dress-up all the time.

REPURPOSE YOUR JEWELRY:

Try using a bejeweled hair clip as a shoe clip or wrapping a necklace around your wrist as a bracelet. Be fearless about wearing jewelry in different ways. How about switching out the chain of your evening bag with a necklace, or adding some charms to it? Just make sure it is strong enough to stay secure. Let your imagination lead you to new and inventive ways to wear what you have.

STACK AND LAYER:

There is a science to creating the perfect stack of bracelets or correctly layering necklaces, rings, etc. I like to call it "jewelryology." It has to do with scale and the

number of pieces that are layered together. You should try to layer your jewelry in odd numbers (i.e., five bracelets, three necklaces, etc.); this assures that there is always a center focal point that is framed by the other pieces. Scale is important in layering as well; accent a larger piece like a medallion pendant with smaller chains and charm necklaces.

The Top Five Pieces Every Girl Needs

....

- Cocktail rings
- Statement earrings
- Hair jewelry
- Stacking bracelets
- Multiple strand necklace

Hair Jewelry

I love making pieces that can be used in multiple ways. This is what led me to create one of my most recognized designs: the Anywhere Clip™. It can be worn as a hair clip, as a brooch, or on your bag, dress, or shoes.

Shoelry

Shoe embellishment dates back to the 1700s when tassels, buckles, bows, and ruffles were all the rage for both ladies and gentlemen. Shoe jewelry or "shoelry" can instantly update or change even the dullest of shoes. Try using hair jewels like the ones we made for Broken Treasure Hair Jewels (page 207) and attach them to the straps. Here are some examples of how we have used Anywhere Clips and other hair accessories to dress up shoes.

Special Occasions

Every day should be a special occasion in the world of wearing jewelry, but some days are extra special. In the past, wearing holiday-themed jewelry might have been something corny that only Aunt Patsy did, showing up for Thanksgiving with her flashing turkey pin and Pilgrim-themed bracelet. Well, why should Aunt Patsy have all the fun? Occasion jewelry is a fun way to celebrate your favorite holidays in style. This doesn't mean resorting to cackling witch earrings on Halloween. This Halloween you can wear your sugar skull bracelets that you made! At Christmastime you can really get creative. Try making earrings out of tiny tree decorations or collage pins and pendants from gift tag art. For other holidays like Independence Day, try stacking your bracelets in the colors of Old Glory.

· CHAPTER 10 ·

Your Jewelry Closet

We're all guilty of letting many of our treasures sink to the bottom of that endless abyss we know as the "junk drawer," or that random basket on the unreachable top shelf of the closet, or the dreaded black hole behind the dresser. To put it simply: if you cannot see your jewels, you'll never wear them! Easy and inspiring access to your jewelry wardrobe is one of the best ways to ensure you'll get plenty of wear out of the jewelry that you're making and buying. I say inspiring because for me, jewelry is artwork, and when it's displayed in fun and imaginative ways, it can really inspire you to create other new pieces. Try organizing your collections in color groups or rainbow order. It's not only pleasing to the eye, but it also makes it easier to find what you need quickly.

I like to think of my closet and dressing area as a dream boutique that I walk into every morning. I am sure it's dreamier in my mind than in real life, but who cares? It's everything I love to wear all in one place. I am constantly moving things around, rearranging and reorganizing my wardrobe and accessories so that I wear everything I have. Try displaying your jewelry on hooks

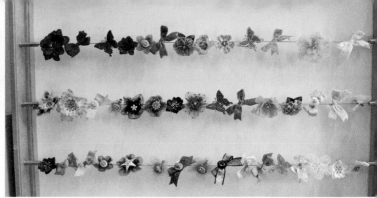

and in see-through acrylic jewelry boxes; being able to see what you have makes it easy to find what you are looking for quickly. Your closet is where you keep all the things you love and treasure, and where you get inspired to play dress-up every day.

Jewelry Organization and Display

Why not use actual displays like the ones in retail stores? Those stores use them for a reason: so that customers can view the collections easily. For our boutiques we had our displays custom made for the most part. But nowadays you can just walk into The Container Store and find amazing jewelry displays. I like things that are non-gimmicky and uncomplicated. Let your jewelry be the focal point of the display, and keep it clean and simple.

NECKLACES:

Busts, dress forms, and dolly heads make great displays for your necklaces. The worst thing you can do is put your necklaces in a drawer together. We all know the tangled sea monster this creates. To avoid a mess, follow this rule: always hang your necklaces whenever possible. I hang my necklaces on actual hangers, then hook them on the wall. For smaller, more delicate pieces, try putting them in clear acrylic divider boxes.

EARRINGS:

There are so many creative ways to display earrings like hanging them around the edge of a jar, or from ribbons tacked across a cork board. But for really easy organizing and to keep your earring pairs together, I love using clear compartment boxes.

RINGS:

You can have a lot of fun displaying your ring collection. My favorite is this gothic skeleton hand candle holder that I have repurposed to collect my cocktail rings. Vintage porcelain glove molds make great ring holders. You can find some great ones on Etsy.

BRACELETS:

Bracelet bars like the ones we use in our boutiques are widely available today. Using these acrylic T-bars keeps your bracelets accessible. My absolute favorite way to store my bracelets is to use sock dividers in my drawers. I stack my bracelets by color or create stacks to wear each day of the week.

HAIR ACCESSORIES:

The best way to keep hair jewelry organized is on a ribbon wrapped canvas or small pillow—and they are so easy to make! Just staple fabric over a canvas and secure the ribbons tightly with hot glue. Hang them on the wall or use a frame easel to display them on your vanity. To make a quick pillow to display your hair jewelry, just take a small, firm, rectangular or square pillow and tie strips of 1" wide ribbon around it. Headbands can be a headache to organize; try stacking them together in a glass bowl.

Caring for Your Jewelry

To keep your jewelry sparkling, use a good-quality polishing cloth. Never put costume jewelry in cleaning solution or under water. This will cause the stones to dull and come loose. Also, you should never store jewelry in bright or direct sunlight as it can cause it to tarnish or fade.

Traveling with Jewelry

Traveling with jewelry can mean breaking your jewelry if you do not pack it properly. I have tried every fancy jewelry roll on the planet, and none works as well as this simple trick. Pack each piece of jewelry separately in a small organza bag and find a sturdy, lightweight box to pack your jewelry bags into. Always put these items in your carry-on (we never check our precious cargo!).

In Closing

My hope is that after you have spent time with this book and made some of the projects, you will be inspired to experiment with your own designs and create something fantastic. Making jewelry for yourself, your family, and friends is not only fun, but it is also incredibly fulfilling when you see how happy something precious that you crafted can make someone feel.

Keep your creativity constantly flowing by setting time aside each week to work on a project. Turn off everything on your mind, shut out the noise, and let yourself work. This is sometimes tough because of our schedules, obligations, and all those electronic gadgets barking at us, but for me it's as important as breathing. It's my personal time to revisit my childhood and my travels, and let the people and experiences that have touched my life inspire my work.

Recently, I took a beautiful trip to a special place in South Carolina called Edisto Island, where my family and I rented a beautiful sea glass blue beach house right on the sand. The first evening we arrived, we all took a walk on the beach at sunset. As the warm tide rolled in around our feet, so did hundreds of seashells. They were mostly abandoned oyster shells in the prettiest shades of pastel pinks, whites, and charcoal grays. As I looked out at the sea, I imagined all the pretty "pearls" that must lie at the bottom decorating the ocean floor, and I let my mind wander. Alfonso looked at me and said, "Tarina, I see the wheels turning"—and he was exactly right. The very first seeds were planted for my spring collection right there on that gorgeous beach.

Let your day-to-day experiences become your design inspirations, and in turn, your pieces will become little historical artifacts of your life. Let your jewelry tell the story of who you are, what inspires you, and what thrills and excites you. And most importantly, always follow your sparkling dreams!

Acknowledgments

From the bottom of my sparkling heart:

Alfonso, my love and my creative partner-in-crime, thanks for believing in me and convincing me to take a chance and embark upon my dreams. Thank you for supporting, protecting, and encouraging me every step of the way. Sharing this adventure with you and the girls by my side is the icing on the cake.

Chloe and Olivia, my sweet, delightful girls, thank you for inspiring me every day with your love, generosity, wit, imagination, and humor. I want to be like you when I grow up.

Mom and Dad, thanks for nurturing my creative spark, curiosity, love of books, art, and music. Most importantly, thank you for teaching me to think independently and march to the beat of my own drum.

Grandpa and Grandma, thank you for being my biggest fans and supporters, and for encouraging me to do what I love so it would never feel like work.

My extraordinary **Team Sparkle** at TARINA TARANTINO, infinite appreciation for your passion and dedication in helping me make the world shine brighter one beautifully crafted piece of jewelry at a time. I couldn't do it without you!

A giant and super glittering thank you to **Ted Max** for your wisdom, guidance, encouragement, and friendship. Heartfelt gratitude to **Sheldon and Peggy Chinsky** for your partnership, belief, support, and kindness.

Thank you to my wonderful photographer, **Kaori Suzuki**, for your beautiful photography, endless calm, and enthusiasm, even on the longest shooting days for this book. Thanks also to the masterful **Albert Sanchez**, who photographed many of the archive editorial images used throughout the book.

I am so grateful to **Running Press**, my editor, **Jordana Tusman**, and **Frances Soo Ping Chow** for your steady guidance, patience, and dedication to the vision of this book. Thank you, **Melissa Gerber**, for the beautiful design execution. Thanks also to **Marc Gerald** and **Sasha Raskin** at The

Agency Group for helping me get this book out of my imagination and onto the page.

Very special thanks to: John Stapleton, Janine Jarman, Judd Minter, Lydia Hearst, Mindy Harper, Sonja Bowers-Teri, Eduardo Campos, Morgen Swenson, Yvonne Montes, Jennifer Vu, Sofia Castelli, Giovanni Volpe, Ann Lopez, Chris Abrego, Blair Sabol, Steven Cojocaru, Margarita Arriagada, Sephora, Laura Takaragawa, Illeana Douglas, Kathy Campos, Michael Gintz, Michael Cho, Steve Hirsh and Cooper Design Space, Rene L'au, Nadja Swarovski, Kelly Osbourne, Debi Mazar, Dakota Fanning, Mindy Kaling, Ethan Eller and The New Mart Building, Tony Rojas, Alison Dickson, Elle Fanning, Larva X, Zelda Williams, Dominik Garcia-Lorido, the Campos family, Aunt Pam, Kristen Robinson, Adam Wallacavage, Brenda Lopez, Arturo Solar, Pedro Zalba, Corinda Cook, Allison Devlin, Jacqueline Tusman, Swarovski, Sanrio, Warner Bros., Kidrobot, and Mattel.

And finally, to our dear and amazing friend **Darren "Daz" Rydstrom**, thank you for always reminding us to stop and smell the roses. We miss you.

Resources

THE BEAD FACTORY

810 S. Maple Avenue

Los Angeles, CA 90014

Tel: 213-624-2121

Fax: 213-624-2127

Web: Beadsfactory.com

The best selection of crystal beads and stones I have ever seen under one roof. Here you can find crystal gemstones in larger sizes and a large assortment of colors. We recommend using this resource for the **Barcelona Slide Cuff (page 111)**. You can also find howlite skull beads for the **Sugar Skull Stretch Bracelet (page 105)**.

BERGER SPECIALTY CO.

113 E. 8th Street

Los Angeles, CA 90014

Tel: 213-627-8783

Fax: 213-680-9743

Web: Bergerbeads.net

A wonderful selection of new and vintage sequins for the **Starlet Sequin Choker (page 95)**, **Kashmir Gypsy Pom-Pom Earrings (page 129)**, and **Mucha Muse Headband (page 213)**.

THE CONTAINER STORE

Web: Containerstore.com

This is the best place to get everything you need for organizing your workspace and jewelry collections. My favorites are the clear acrylic jewelry displays and hinged acrylic compartment boxes.

EASTERN FINDINGS CORP.

116 County Courthouse Road

Garden City Park, NY 11040

Tel: 1-800-332-6640

Fax: 516-747-6650

Web: Easternfindings.com

A comprehensive assortment of materials, especially metal findings, including metal beads for the **Techno Tribal Pin Collar (page 87)**, eye screw bails for the **Tokyo Toy Store Matinee Necklace (page 67)**, and French-style barrettes for the **Broken Treasure Hair Jewels (page 207)**.

EBAY

Web: ebay.com

A great place to hunt for the treasures you will need to make the **Broken Treasure Hair Jewels (page 207)**. Try a search for "broken vintage jewelry." People even sell it on eBay by the pound! You can also find Koko and Tara plastic baby barrettes for the **Sweet Shop Earrings (page 143)** and **Fantastic Plastic Mod Ring (page 173)**, and a variety of cameos for the **Acid Cameo Western Belt Buckle (page 223)**.

HAR-MAN IMPORTING CORP.

95 Bi-County Boulevard

Farmingdale, NY 11735

Tel: 631-756-9800

Fax: 631-756-9845

Web: Shopharmanbeads.com

A wonderful resource including Swarovski crystal beads and stones in all sizes for the **City Girl Hoop Earrings (page 149)**, and all kinds of amazing beads including a great selection of wooden beads for the **Cinnamon Girl Bib Necklace (page 77)**.

HORD CRYSTAL CORPORATION

45 York Avenue

Pawtucket, RI 02860

Tel: 1-800-444-2989

Fax: 401-723-3036

Web: Hordcrystal.com

The finest crystal chain with the widest range of sizes for the **Petit Chapeau (page 197)** and the **Broken Treasure Hair Jewels (page 207)**.

JAPANESE ERASER MUSEUM

Web: Erasermuseum.com

Toy erasers in endless colors and themes for the **Tokyo Toy Store Matinee Necklace (page 67)**.

JO-ANN FABRIC AND CRAFT STORES

Web: Joann.com

Jo-Ann has a great selection of buttons for the **Strange Delight Earrings (page 137)**, **Fantastic Plastic Mod Ring (page 173)**, and **Sweet Shop Earrings (page 143)**, feathers and appliqués for the **Petit Chapeau (page 197)**, and felt fabric for the **Dollhouse Flowerpot Ring (page 159)**.

KIDROBOT

Web: Kidrobot.com

I love Kidrobot, because it has the ultimate collection of blind box vinyl toys like the ones I used in the **Tokyo Toy Store Matinee Necklace (page 67)**.

M&J TRIMMING

1008 Sixth Avenue

New York, NY 10018

Web: Mjtrim.com

This is a great resource that has chains, sequins, buttons, crystals, and more, including sequin flower trim by the yard for **Starlet Sequin Choker (page 95)**.

POLYFORM PRODUCTS COMPANY

Web: Sculpey.com

Some great essentials for your polymer clay projects including all sculpting tools and clay supplies needed for the **Paris Apartment Cocktail Ring (page 181)**, **Barcelona Slide Cuff (page 111)**, and the **Acid Cameo Western Belt Buckle (page 223)**.

RENAISSANCE RIBBONS

Tel: 530-692-0842

Fax: 530-692-0915

Web: Renaissanceribbons.com

Gorgeous French-milled ribbon and trim in a stunning array of colors and styles. The best part is that most of their ribbons only have a one-yard minimum. We recommend using this resource for the **Bow Tie Bangle (page 119)**, **Petit Chapeau (page 197)**, and **Mucha Muse Headband (page 213)**.

SAVE ON CRAFTS

Tel: 831-768-8428

Web: Save-on-crafts.com

Vintage inspired flowers and velvet leaves for the **Mucha Muse Headband (page 213)** and exquisite feather hat trims for the **Petit Chapeau (page 197)**.

STAMPENDOUS

1122 N. Kraemer Place

Anaheim, CA 92806

Tel: 1-800-869-0474

Fax: 1-800-578-2329

Web: Stampendous.com

Very high-quality, reusable one-ounce needle-tip plastic gluing bottles.

STANFRE INDUSTRIES, INC.

19 W. 36th Street, Floor 6

New York, NY 10018

Tel: 1-888-223-5223

Web: Stanfreind.com

A unique and high-quality selection of chain for the **Tokyo Toy Store Matinee Necklace (page 67)**, Lucite beads for the **Techno Tribal Pin Collar (page 87)** and **Jubilee Stretch Ring (page 189)**, and plenty of cabochons, stones, and findings. The owner is one of the kindest and most knowledgeable people in the jewelry supplies industry. If he doesn't have it, he will point you in the right direction.

TANDY LEATHER FACTORY

Web: Tandyleatherfactory.com

A nice selection of rolled edge western buckle blanks and tooled leather belt straps for the **Acid Cameo Western Belt Buckle (page 223)**.

TARINA TARANTINO/THE SPARKLE FACTORY

Web: Tarinatarantino.com

Here you can find The Sparkle Factory by Tarina Tarantino collection including jewelry tools and findings like **The Sparkle Factory Magic Wand (page 44)**, earring posts with 6mm dapped cup for the **Kashmir Gypsy Pom-Pom Earrings (page 129)**, the ring shank with ½-inch gluing pad for the **Fantastic Plastic Mod Ring (page 173)**, the gun-metal ornate loop pendant for the **Mucha Muse Headband (page 213)**, and more. You can also see our latest jewelry, accessory, and beauty collections.

Photo Credits

Kaori Suzuki: Cover and all interior photography with exception to the following:

Albert Sanchez: pp. 8, 9, 25 (Tarina portrait), 33 (ruby headphones), 83, 92-93, 97, 121, 134, 154-155, 161, 170-171, 175, 199, 238, 241-248

Adam Wallacavage: pp. 75 (Barbie vanity), 254 (Barbie display case)

Alexander Lipkin: pp. 209 (hair jewelry), 213 (wonderland muse), 245 (Illeana Mod – upper right)

Donato Sardella: p. 24 (Los Angeles store)

Aaron Cobbett: pp. 225 (Barbie belt), 245 (Barbie shoe)

Valerie Macon/Getty Images: p. 240 (Tarina red carpet)

Darren Rydstrom: p. 259 (Edisto beach)

Tarina Tarantino's personal collection: pp. 10, 14, 17, 28 (butterfly sketch), 31 (mood board), 32 (toy shelf and nesting dolls), 34, 36-37, 41 (treasure boxes), 62-63 (beads/cabochons, mood board, notebook, and Tarina sketching), 69, 73, 111 (Park Güell), 129, 135, 156-157, 181, 252-258

Index